About the Author

Author Jennifer Aves is a seasoned Canadian graphic designer who shapeshifted with the help of her many wholistic modalities into an energetic wellness business owner and author. Bringing along with her all of her creativity and fire to infuse each session and word with a positive reiki spark. Fuelling her mission of creating unconditional love, one positive sparked page at a time. Nowadays you can find her on Lake Simcoe embracing her love for cold plunging, paddle boarding and swimming as she continues to give through wellness and creativity.

Key Reset

How I fixed my sh*tty attitude by finding my spark of joy from within

Jennifer Aves

Key Reset

How I fixed my sh*tty attitude by finding my spark
of joy from within

Vanguard Press

VANGUARD PAPERBACK

© Copyright 2025
Jennifer Aves

Cover photograph by **Sandra Leitch** @shootingmonsters

The right of Jennifer Aves to be identified as author of this work has been asserted by her in accordance with the Copyright, Designs and Patents Act 1988.

All Rights Reserved

No reproduction, copy or transmission of this publication may be made without written permission.
No paragraph of this publication may be reproduced, copied or transmitted save with the written permission of the publisher, or in accordance with the provisions of the Copyright Act 1956 (as amended).

Any person who commits any unauthorised act in relation to this publication may be liable to criminal prosecution and civil claims for damages.

A CIP catalogue record for this title is available from the British Library.

ISBN 978 1 80016 788 9

*Vanguard Press is an imprint of
Pegasus Elliot Mackenzie Publishers Ltd.*
www.pegasuspublishers.com

First Published in 2025

**Vanguard Press
Sheraton House Castle Park
Cambridge England**

Printed & Bound in Great Britain

Dedicated to myself for waking up early and wanting more. The purpose of my journey was to figure out how to dig in, grow, and feel. To share, give, and let go. Discovering how to fix my shitty attitude and what it meant to experience real emotions in the moment. To open myself up to truly sharing. Ultimately to give myself permission to figure out how to receive and let go all at the same time. Developing freely into an awakened spirit whose reality of fun, and a newfound spark of joy could be felt each waking day. Inviting anyone who is on their own personal journey to join me, hopefully sparking a brighter light from within.

Acknowledgements

Tool reference and gratitude:
Tools I used for awakening my spark and opening my mind: Abraham (Ester Hicks) — *Ask and it is Given* Bob Proctor — *Mind Movies* Dr Bradley Nelson — *Emotion Code* for helping me learn how to release trapped emotions.

Dr Joe Dispenza — *Becoming Supernatural. Breaking the Habit of Being Yourself. You are the Placebo.*

Gabby Bernstein — for my buddy Sandra who gave me the *Universe has your back* book which changed the course of my life. Gabby for your truly inspiring book and your beautiful *Super Attractor Cards* which have carried my family and me through many rough days and difficult decisions.

Jake Ducey — *Self-Hypnosis* for helping to break past conditioning while I slept.

Jay Shetty — *Think Like a Monk* for bringing me into the present moment

Christine — *Quantum Therapy*. Tools I used for boosting my immune system and dealing with anxiety: Mel Robbins — For your *5, 4, 3, 2, 1 Method*, Mel and her son's car banter on Instagram priceless. Robin Sharma — *5 a.m. Club*.

Wim Hof Method App — For helping me push past fear by using your insightful breathing, and cold therapy not to mention the reminder to just breathe mother fucker!

Tools I used for healing: *Balance Health Wellness Music* — For giving me a positive outlet to create something positive in a time when the world was turned upside down. *Mei-Ian YouTube* — Your angelic voice allowed for many, many shifts. Mother Nature — Unconditional love. Best for last *many, many, many thanks* to:

Kevin — For motivating me to go within! Makayla — For reminding me daily that you should never take life too seriously and to continually feed creativity. Spencer — For your old man's wisdom, witty jokes, and many stories. Friends and family — For those who positively impacted and continue to support my journey. Shelley and Heather — For your gracious edits and feedback. Sandra for your incredible photography skills and support. My Parents — Diane and Al, it is through all my experiences that have made me the powerful woman I am today. Covid dedication: To all those who lost loved ones and to those who have tirelessly worked through this pandemic my spark of light goes out to you. Pegasus Publishing/Vanguard Press staff who helped bring this book to life. Universe — For always and unconditionally being there for me. Myself — For waking up and wanting more even if it meant in the darkness. Sparking a light from within.

Contents

CHAPTER 1 ....
365 days to heal myself 13
CHAPTER 2 ....
365 days to what? 21
CHAPTER 3 ....
No time, except for excuses 47
CHAPTER 4 ....
Fixing my shitty attitude 66
CHAPTER 5 ....
Ninety percent fear. 76
CHAPTER 6 ....
Make the damn choice. 101
CHAPTER 7 ....
To forgive or not to forgive, that is the question. 118
CHAPTER 8 ....
Never underestimate the power of a good poop. 142
CHAPTER 9 ....
Is there more than one way to peel and eat a banana? 158
CHAPTER 10 ....
Five A.M. reality call. Get the fuck up! 176
CHAPTER 11 ....
You are never too old for a good fart joke. 193
CHAPTER 12 ....
Guilty till proven innocent. 216
CHAPTER 13 ....
The taste of disappointment. 224
CHAPTER 14 ....
I am. 236

CHAPTER 15 ....
365 days to heal. 248
Contract to myself: 254
To-Do-List: 255

CHAPTER 1

365 days to heal myself

The underlying sadness seems to always be there, lingering around me as an unwanted friend with hands gripped tightly on my wrist. Why, why are you holding on to me? Why am I not able to release you?

As I lay in bed tonight contemplating my day and the way it unfolded, the sadness grips tighter. It pierces right through the warmth of my husband lying next to me, its stinging icy grip piercing its way deep into my very being. I know in my heart there must be more, to feel more and to be more. More than this overwhelming sadness.

For the longest time, I believed that life is a struggle and that it takes hard work and perseverance to be successful. I had exhausted myself with this flawed concept of working hard, pushing through, and reaching goals. Only to be left with gripping sadness and an overwhelming feeling of never being satisfied and never enough, as I repeated this process again and again. Somehow expecting to feel different or better as each goal was achieved. Instead, a deep sadness accompanied each milestone, and I continued to feel empty and alone.

Over the past ten years, I had tried to remedy my endless sadness with as many tools and methods as I could consume. Searching for the golden key to release sadness's death grip, I began devouring as much inspiration, meditation, yoga, mantras, manifesting, self-help books, videos, and podcasts as humanly possible. Going so far as to get certified in massage therapy, reiki, reflexology, and colour therapy. Still, the grip of sadness held firm, tightening its hold a little more each time.

Sure, I had rare glimpses of happiness for short periods of time. Gratefulness would wash over me and then, all too quickly, sadness would abruptly tighten its grip and yank me off my feet again.

It had been a tireless search for true happiness. The happiness and joy that came when things were quiet, and life slowed down. Instead of the constant undertone of sadness and disappointment in myself and others. Or worse when sadness seemed to be present for no reason at all. The kind of sadness that loved to linger, with icy roots that pierced deep. I often wondered if anyone else felt the same. The same all-consuming sadness for no apparent reason or if it was just me. I looked for a cure in the form of more success, acknowledgement, attention, perfection, and ultimately more love.

I felt a deep drive to chase real happiness and believed in my heart there was a way to overcome my sorrow. There had to be more to life. More than having sadness show up at every occasion. I knew I could not exist like this any longer. A big change was necessary.

That is when it happened, one frigid cold winter evening I decided I had enough. It had been a week from hell, of feeling alone in a house full of people, and I knew I had hit my breaking point. Everything seemed to be going wrong compounded by a constant stream of arguing within my family. As I attempted to talk with people who never seemed to be listening. Ask for things that never seemed to be done. Express my feelings only to be told I was overreacting. Only to leave me lying here in the darkness with a deep-seated feeling of sadness and overwhelming anger as the resentment stiffened its way across my chest.

All I could think of is why. Why is this happening to me?

Sure, I may have a super short temper and the uncanny ability to freak out over the smallest of details leaving me dumbfounded as to why no one else cared as much as I did. This, paired with a strong sense that everyone was working against me, often left me to wonder if I was losing my mind or if I simply just needed to take a break. Maybe a few days away would do me some good. Maybe I could check myself into a hotel or borrow a friend's cottage for a few days to regroup and refresh. I had mulled over this fantasy so many times but tonight for the first time I knew in my heart that this fantasy get-a-way would fix nothing.

Even though I still craved an escape for a few days, today would be the day I decided to just stop. Stop and commit to staying and go all in. I was utterly exhausted from sadness, and it was time to stop running, pull up my big girl panties, and take off these running shoes forever.

As I drifted off to sleep feeling somewhat relieved and overwhelmed with the unknown.

I awoke to a fresh new day unfolding much like a beautiful flower opening for the first time on a warm spring morning. I started to understand and accept my reality. I had a family that loved me. Period. A family that loved me no matter what story I created in my mind about no one listening, no one helping, no one understanding me or no one really loving me. I realised that even with all the love in the world from my family it would never be enough unless I started to look within. I knew the key to freeing myself from constant sadness was possibly in my reach.

Searching for that magic key for a solution in books, videos, podcasts, careers, or anything which focused on positive change. So, why was today like no other day I had experienced? Why was it so life-changing? I did not win big on the lottery but it damn near felt like I had. A pivotal feeling washed over me of no longer wanting to run and realising that although I had gorged on all these amazing self-help tools, I had not actually put them into practice.

Sure, I would have momentary inspiration which even evoked a strong positive emotion but that would be the extent of it. Basically, what I had been doing was the equivalent to researching countless hours on how to fix a broken car, but never actually rolling up my sleeves to fix my car. Or getting excited over scrolling through numerous and delicious recipes, only to never end up making or tasting one scrumptious dish.

I had all the tools and love right in front of me. The question was whether I would fix the damn car, bake the damn recipe, or fix my damn self by slugging my way out of the mud.

The very brutal realisation that I never used or implemented any of these tools to help myself hit me like a ton of bricks. Constantly inspired by new revelations for three seconds of my day only to be left searching for something more. Constantly searching, constantly starving, and constantly sad. Today was different because of the simple acknowledgement of my feverous consumption. A consumption of self-help materials which I abruptly purged as fast as I consumed them, giving me momentary relief and satisfaction.

I realised I had become a self-help bulimic. I didn't stop to chew, swallow, and let the information fuel my body, mind, and spirit. I didn't use any of these tools for daily growth, which ultimately left me stuck where I was in a state of perpetual sadness.

Enough. No more false promises to myself, of teasing fulfilment with self-help knowledge that was never put into action. There would be no more starving my spirit of lasting joy, while all the ingredients for a wonderful 10-course meal were at hand. Change was here today, whether I was ready, or not. The only problem was that first, I had to do the work. This meal needed to be prepared, cooked and served before I could enjoy it. The resounding question — was I ready — thundered through my mind.

I *was*, committing to myself: that I would no longer be tolerating breadcrumbs when it came to all the abundance and love that I deserved.

The meal my spirit now demanded was unbelievably detailed. I knew it would take real work to create it. As I started to create a menu and plan of action that had the ability to heal my spirit. A plan, I quickly realised, was also going to take time. Time, effort, and commitment. Three hundred and sixty-five days of time, effort, and commitment to be exact.

One full year to feed my spirit and heal myself seemed reasonable. Three hundred and sixty-five days to find my spark of lasting happiness and release this underlying grip of sadness forever. This would be the biggest commitment I had ever made to myself. Now having reached the other side successfully I hope as you follow my journey as it may help and inspire you to do the same.

Keep in mind my timeline is not your timeline though. Maybe your commitment is two weeks or two years. That's something I cannot dictate for you. But what I do know for sure is that this was a life-changing commitment, so pivotal and freeing that I felt a dire need to share this journey. So, believe me when I say take the leap of faith to look within yourself as I share my journey with you. Together we have the capacity to create positive change within ourselves, which creates a beautiful ripple effect outward to those around us. Others who themselves see and sense a change cannot help but to evolve in a positive way as well.

So, there on that cold winter evening when my real awakening started, there was an excitement but also a worry. I recognized that this moment too could be one of those fleeting inspirations I'd experienced in the past. So, I took charge, got off the couch, and I wrote a contract with myself. It had only one simple yet powerful statement: Take every positive lesson learned and implement it into my day.

I, Jennifer Aves, am open to growing, healing, and learning over the next three hundred and sixty-five days. By taking every positive tool learned I will implement it into every moment of every day while I continue to grow towards a happy and fulfilled life of love.
— Jennifer Aves.

CHAPTER 2

365 days to what?

Sounds simple enough... Yay! Go me... I got this... As my internal pep talk kicks in, I try to convince myself that healing is possible as a sense of doubt weasels its way in. It does, doesn't it... Right... R.I.G.H.T...

A serious reality check would need to take place, a reality check on myself. Not on my work, my husband, my kids, my family, my parents, or my friends. A reality check on me and only me.

This thought may scare the crap out of you. It definitely scared the crap out of me and excited me all at the same time. I knew that if I genuinely wanted to release this death grip of underlying sadness it had something to do with my mind, my body, and my soul connection.

After all, I was the only constant thing throughout my life that transpired to be at every happy and sad event over the years. You know that saying?

Quoted by an unknown: "If you run into an asshole in the morning you ran into an asshole. If you run into assholes all day, you're the asshole".

I was the constant, I was that asshole, so to fix my sadness I would have to fix *me*, not anyone else.

Just me, but what did I get myself into and how was I going to pull off healing my spirit and ultimately myself? Little did I know that this deep seeded sadness was only going to be the tip of the iceberg. In order for this to work I would need to check in on my mindset to make sure I was being honest with myself.

As I ventured into day one of healing, I found myself at a crossroads trying to determine just which path I was going to take. A reality check of sorts. A reality check in which I would frequently use to gauge the direction which would best advance my personal growth. This reality check acted like a compass aiding to keep the focus on myself as I was notorious for looking outward and playing the blaming game. Losing sight of moving forward often stuck or even making my way backwards. This compass utilised these reality checks to help guide me, ultimately maintaining my accountability to this healing contract.

The only rule that mattered now, was to be open and transparent with myself as I followed this compass.

Reality check in

Mind check-in.

I mainly feel unsatisfied and sad with a mix of mood swings and negative emotions. Flying off the handle over small stuff regularly. Super irritated, never satisfied.

Body check-in.

Tired a lot. Trying to work out. Currently sleeping in until the last possible moment after numerous snoozes. Feeling blah.

Spirit check-in.

Feeling disconnected. Not sure where to go from here.

OK, here we go. Now that my first reality check is done, I quickly realised I might need more like three hundred and sixty-five thousand days to navigate my way to healing. Baby steps I remind myself. You got this, try to think positive, I repeat over and over in my head giving myself a little pep talk.

Three hundred and sixty-five days is more than enough time to find some kind of spark that will bring my mind, body, and soul together for an amazing kick-ass party. However, right now, I acknowledge. I feel more like the world's biggest party pooper comparable to a little piglet screeching away stuck in the mud waiting to be rescued.

After all, piglets do love the mud. Did I love the messy chaos of life and the feelings of being stuck? Hell no!

Or did I, was I more comfortable slugging through life acknowledging that when life appeared easy and carefree it had an undertone that something had to be wrong with all this ease. That good feelings and good things never lasted.

As I sat in the thick dense mud of my life knowing that no one was coming to rescue me. Feeling stuck I decided to just sit and take a moment, a moment to reflect. At that moment I knew what was needed.

Step one would require an understanding and acknowledgment of what I truly, honestly believed in. A step which is imperative to any personal growth journey. Knowing that the only right answer is the one you find from within oneself.

OK, I thought. *If I am to truly go within, I need to sort out a few of the fundamentals. Fundamentals like what the hell do I even believe in?* After much contemplation (and a nap or two later), a solid unshakable belief formed.

One simple fundamental belief: I believe that an awe-inspiring positive energy exists within each person. A positive energy facilitated and powered through our actions, words and thoughts of unconditional love.

I wholeheartedly believe this to be true however, I also acknowledged that I did not trust this positive energy to be there for me. Especially in an unconditional kind of way. OK, this is good, I remind myself. Do not judge, just keep digging. So where did this belief in polar opposites of positive energy and distrust come from? Distrust was an easy one to pinpoint, my childhood. Childhood as an answer may sound so cliche, and you may even be rolling your eyes. Hear me out as I share my journey. It contained so much validity to it that it cannot be ignored. OK, so where did belief in positive energy come from?

My mind starts to dig through its memory archives of growing up in a Ukrainian Catholic church. Memories flooding back of our parish losing a loving spirited priest who always smiled and made church enjoyable. He was transferred to a new parish, and we were now being blessed with someone who was quite the opposite. As the thoughts of disappointment come rushing back, even though I attended those Sunday masses with my parents, and completed all the sacraments, it still never felt like it was the right place for me. The underlying messages of intolerance and judgement were constantly being preached. I would now spend the hour sitting on the hard wooden pew attempting to block out the words of intolerance as my mind escaped into my own dreams.

Contemplating my master plan of how I could avoid going to hell for being a sinner. Not to mention, all those poor souls, who did not even attend church. Some days I even wished I were one of those poor souls just so that I did not have to be here. Even if it meant my impending doom, according to the church.

One Sunday morning as I sat there in church, I found myself zoning out. Dreaming of a place of love and guidance. A place where people were excited to be there with smiles on their faces. Excited to shake hands and actually look at each other. A place where I could sing freely and smile freely. Even spend the whole hour admiring the beautiful painting on the ceiling if I felt like it, instead of being scolded that it was rude. I found myself constantly searching for answers, ultimately searching for acceptance and love.

I sensed a small spark of hope that there had to be something more out there. Even at ten years old I could not wait to grow up and make a better life for myself. So, every Sunday after that, I would bask in my one hour of dreaming up a positive new life for myself. Sixty minutes dedicated to one focused dream of finding love and acceptance. As my dream hour would come to an end, I knew in these moments that there was power in positive actions to raise positive people to do positive things.

However, as the years passed, I began struggling my way through my teens. My dreams of creating a positive life for myself somehow appeared to have dwindled away, along with our Sunday church attendance.

Knowing that my day of freedom would eventually come, but when? The sheer length of this part of my journey seemed to be never-ending. My very existence at this time seemed to be hyper-focused on the countdown to my great escape to freedom.

Two more years, one more year, almost there. I would continually remind myself that the emergence of this glorious life would only be experienced once I moved out and onto my own. some days it seemed like more than I could bear. Tirelessly waiting and searching for more as I walked on eggshells so as to not rock the boat. Feeding into my need to be a people pleaser. These years resulted in an overwhelming build-up of anger, resentment, sadness, and loneliness. My relationship and connection to myself was often stretched to its limits. Leaving me to search for love and acceptance anywhere I could find it. Like most teens, I was looking for love in all the wrong places, as the song goes.

Often mistaking sex and alcohol for true connection and love, constantly craving that closeness but never feeling it. While other times I had found glimmers of happiness, peace, and joy. Speckled amongst those peaceful coveted moments of happiness spent with family and close friends rekindled a spark of faith in positive people and life. Fondly recalling those long summer days swimming and playing at the lake. This small spark would light up and go out just as fast as the years passed. Lighting up hope, on and off, on and off.

Finally, that fateful day had come. I had somehow managed to make it out on my own as a first-year university student. My time was filled with freedom, laughter, friends, parties, and alcohol. Especially alcohol, the never-ending flow of alcohol. Drinking was nothing new to me, as growing up with an alcoholic had its perks. Since I had started to consume alcohol around age twelve and quickly became well versed in drinking this was one of those perks. Perks to mastering the task of where to get alcohol, who could get it, and even what my alcoholic drink of choice already was. Spending much of my teens wasted and or vomiting from alcohol poisoning almost every other weekend. So, this transition to a typical university life of drinking was an easy one for me.

The first few months of university blurred by until one fateful morning while getting ready for class a voice stopped me in my tracks. Which was perfect timing, as this whole booze induced lifestyle was getting me nowhere. I was exhausted. Exhausted from the party scene. Tired of feeling tired. Noticing that each time it was taking me more and more alcohol to feel anything that resembled happiness. Or at least what I perceived as happiness at the time.

This particular morning started off pretty much the same as every morning. I got ready for my class, nursed my pounding hangover, and then proceeded to mull over in my mind the chaos that had ensued from the night before. As feelings of guilt rushed in from getting drunk and choices made. There was nothing new about this familiar dysfunctional cycle. Drink and feel better, drink more, get drunk, pass out, wake up, feel worse, feel guilty, and then repeat.

I was so exhausted from this never-ending cycle, and that is when it happened.

In one split moment... my mind veered away from the cycle of guilty toxic thoughts. A voice rumbled within me that felt like it stopped time and burned through my soul.

It said, '*Why?*'... *Why, what?* I thought to myself. '*Why?*'... it said again. 'Why am I *still* doing this if I no longer lived at home anymore?'

I had never asked myself this before. There have been so many other questions such as "why is this happening to me" or "why does no one love me?"

It was at that very moment that time stood still. With its fiery breath, it burned right through me. Releasing a searing ball of emotion scorching through my skin. Singeing my ribs as it impacted the centre of my heart, knocking the wind right out of my body.

I felt as if my fiery ten-year-old self appeared before me morphing into a dragon as she discharged that fireball with those words directing it into my heart as it shocked me out of my numbed present state of mind. Igniting the memory of that pivotal day in church when I vowed to her to make a better life for myself.

As I sat on the end of my bed, now uncontrollably crying holding myself as the deep burning emotion turned to actual physical pain in my chest. Thoughts blasted through my mind of wonder if this pain was indeed a heart attack. Instantly, I began to laugh almost in a hysterical state as I admitted to myself that this was by no means a real heart attack.

For once in a very long time, I realised that I was in fact allowing myself to feel.

To truly feel all of the pain, anger and sorrow acknowledging that the numbing effect of last night's alcohol had fully worn off. These raw emotions were creating physical pain as they were released with each spiritual wave. Tears of relief and the most bizarre guttural sounds vibrated from my body. I vividly remember this moment as I rocked myself back and forth bawling and laughing just allowing everything to flow. Shocked by the sounds and sensations coming from my very being.

At that very moment, I promised myself to never choose the path of an alcoholic. To choose me, to never stop trying to find my spark no matter what it took.

I stood up from my bed feeling as if it was the first day of my life that I was standing up for myself literally and figuratively. Pretty much like Wonder Woman with her all-powerful cape flapping in the wind but with a serious hangover, tear drenched shirt and sweatpants.

I then made my way to the university, sort of shocked that I still decided to go to class that day. Admitting to myself I had already skipped a few classes for little to no reason. But yet here I am. It really was just shy of a Christmas miracle after the morning I just experienced. Basking in my newfound Wonder Woman-like power adorning my red cape and seriously red puffy eyes due to the therapeutic yet very, very ugly cry I had just experienced. I made my way relishing in a newfound shift of reconnecting with myself. Zipping through the halls to my world religion class, catching a reflection of my own face in the window along the corridor. Even through my red puffy eyes, I could see something new in myself. Something I had not seen for an exceptionally long time.

I witnessed pride. Pride behind those red puffy eyes as I continued down the corridor taking in a deep breath basking in the forgotten feelings of being proud of oneself.

Rounding the corner and entering my now-packed world religion lecture I took my seat. As the realisation that the first half of the semester had been wasted on me or maybe I was just wasted. Either way, I was not really sure. I had seriously been contemplating dropping this terrible class recalling all the excuses I had dreamt up for myself. Over the past few months excuses over why this class sucked so badly. Excuses why my prof's accent was making the content of the class too hard to understand even if I wanted to. Or my favourite excuse — "what does this guy even know about religion?"

Now fully aware of my own toxic excuses, a massive grin of self-awareness came over me. Like a little kid not knowing the contents of a present before they were allowed to bust into it. All these ridiculous excuses suddenly subsided and feelings of being gifted a magic key that had the ability to open up my mind was found within that precious package. With one quick turn of that magic golden key, my mind was open.

I then continued reading my textbook along with my prof as he spoke each word, my mind began to unlock and relax a little more. It felt like a lifetime ago to release the tension in order to experience a peaceful mind. Especially relaxed to a place where I could finally experience that warm spark in my chest again. *Wow*, I thought twice in one day. *I really am wonder woman!*

The semester continued and so did my newfound understanding of religions, methodologies, and mindsets. The deeper I dug into a spiritual way of oneness, the more it piqued my interest. Could this be real? Is this too good to be true? Could there possibly be a simple way that focused on pure positive thinking, positive speaking, and positive acting? An equal oneness that was not full of power mongering fear tactics. A oneness which inspired and taught all people that positive energy is found within each one of us with a sole purpose of evolving a person into the best version of themselves as we contribute to the spark of collective consciousness.

Soon after this revelation of amazing possibilities for freedom, the serious grip of sadness and loneliness overtook me once again. Frankly, I was really pissed off to still be having all these deep feelings of sadness. After all, I was free. I am choosing life by moving on to something better. Why is making this colossal life-changing choice not enough?

I had dreamt of this day for years. Now that it was here, I was left feeling more confused than ever. Eventually leaving me to stare right in the face of all these feelings. Terrible ugly feelings. Horribly intense feelings of anger, sadness, blame, and guilt. Either way, I knew I could not continue my life numbing myself with alcohol. Even if this meant I had no choice but to comb my way through every shitty uncomfortable feeling that I was faced with or had stuffed down into the depths of my being.

The years passed and the journey of combing my way through my feelings began. Throughout my twenties and well into my thirties, this process would be slow and tedious. A process that would take time and patience. Much akin to combing through a head of lice. I know gross, right? You know it must be done, but you really do not want to do it. You may even put it off denying that it is in fact happening to you. It looks and sounds disgusting, yet you just cannot seem to look away. However, *damn*, you feel so relieved when it is done.

Obviously, this was a slow, difficult, gross time in my journey. Even my disgusting choice of how to share this part of my life describes it to a tee. Learning that using time, humour, and vigilance to do and face difficult gross emotional situations would aid in slowly moving me forward with the help of a few close friends and family.

So as the years passed and my journey of going within continued, I could clearly feel sadness lingering at each turn. Tightening its grip more than not. Be that as it may, I only felt comfortable scraping the surface of my emotions. Often jokingly yelling *"Serenity now"* inspired by George from Seinfeld who apparently was also on his own healing journey but not seriously working at it either.

I had spent these years constantly pushing through as I meandered my way from University to college to a seven-year career at the Edmonton Journal. Topping it all off with one brief engagement and marriage that lasted only a couple of years. As my sole prerequisite in choosing a lifelong partner was that he not be an alcoholic, hence our relationship was destined to fail. Whereas most newlyweds were inseparable love birds we were either avoiding one another or busy bringing out the worst in each other.

My philosophy at the time was "go big or go home" often triggered screaming matches and ultimately resulted in me locking myself in the bathroom unable to articulate what I was truly feeling or needing. Only to then slink my way-out tucked tail as I condescendingly apologised that it was all my fault. Spiralling more guilt and resentment into our already doomed relationship and at that moment I understood that it always takes two to tango if you know what I mean.

Therefore, if I was going to go, I was going to go big. I had to go all in because I sure as hell was not going to move back home. Once again, I had hit my breaking point wondering how yet again after all these years, had I ended up searching for love in all the wrong places.

As I walked out that day to leave my marriage of two years, I topped it off by quitting my steady job and enrolling myself into Massage Therapy school. Without resentment but a clear knowing that we seemed to have brought out the worst in each other, we parted ways, and my holistic pursuit of positive energy and wellness began. Reminding me that I did have the power to create a spark from within even if I had no idea how to use or access it on a consistent basis.

To most bystanders, this 'seemingly' rapid choice to leave my marriage and work stunned everyone including my then husband. 'Seemingly', being the keyword as most decisions once I eventually acted on were backed by years of internal conflict and indecision. Cycling through mind games with myself of 'should I stay, or should I go' or 'why did I get married in the first place'. Confirming the statistical fact that many women leave their marriage emotionally well before that fateful day they physically walk out that door.

As friends rushed in to help me with a place to stay and promises of feeling better warmed my heart. The glorious warmth of my spark could be felt as it lasted that entire day, that is, until I laid down to go to sleep. The rush of emotions and guilt began to flood in. As my old friend sadness relentlessly began to tighten its grip reminding me of the cold hard facts: I was now homeless, unemployed, broke and soon to be divorced. These thoughts instantly triggered an ugly cry. As I cried myself to sleep with my face buried in my pillow so as to not burden my friends with the sounds of my deep seeded sorrow I drifted in and out of sleep.

I awoke to a glorious warmth crossing over my chest. I managed to open my tear-crusted puffy eyes glancing down as I was greeted with a ray of sunshine glistening through the slightly parted curtains that hung over the window. I felt gratitude for having that little ray of light touch my heart sparking the light of a new day and new beginnings.

The solution is simple I told myself, even though I was waking up from a half-assed sleep of tossing and turning for hours still I had a reassuring sense that everything would be ok. My mind started to formulate a plan. I will just get a part-time job, even wait tables if I need to, put myself through school and just live frugally in an affordable place or something along those lines.

My guardian angels must have existed within that glorious beam of sunlight as my plans all came together in a matter of days. I found myself carrying in a load of moving boxes as I entered my new bachelor suite apartment as life aligned itself with positive energy blazing.

Even now recalling all the fond memories of how cosy my sweet little apartment was, I relished in my newfound freedom and admitted to myself just how far I had come. This new space I called home was not just filled with peace, laughing, and healing it would also provide me with a safe place where I could secretly sulk around my apartment for weeks on end feeling sorry for myself. Feeding into my own pity party as I binged on bags of Oreo cookies and licked my wounds.

Knowing full well that if I left the safety of my sacred space a negative wave of energy would be felt. It was as if a megaphone had been sounded as I exited my apartment complex. Blasting an ear-shattering announcement, ' *Look* at the giant scarlet letter on her'. 'CAPITAL D'. 'A big red D for divorce'. 'Miss Di-vorce-a what a failure'. 'Make way she is coming through'. As my catholic guilt would get the best of me causing me to then scramble back to the secure confines of my apartment.

The crazy thing with big choices and moving out on your own is that the focus is now all on you. There is no longer anyone to blame, argue with, or support you. This dark awareness triggered a massive backslide as I hurled myself directly into old habits of overindulging in alcohol in order to drown out my sorrows. Only this time I would recognize the signs and remind myself to make better choices.

The long and short of it was I ended up waiting on tables as I put myself through school. Frequently visited our local pub with a girlfriend as we danced and attempted to not drink our faces off. Often reassuring ourselves that we were there to dance not to get drunk which was another one of those saving graces. We also loved to play a little game of 'what about him' as she pointed out cute single guys on the dance floor. I would just roll my eyes and laugh as I made up as many irrational asinine excuses as I could muster like 'nope, I don't like shoes', or 'no, I don't like his belt' resulting in more giggles. Frankly, I just kept telling myself I would rather be alone for the rest of my life than be with someone who brought out the worst in me.

Soon after this declaration of spinsterhood, if need be, I called up my girlfriend and convinced her to go dancing yet again at our local neighbourhood pub. That night seemed to be much like all the other outings we had taken together. We would have one drink and then switch to a soda or cranberry juice, which funny enough would appear as if we were still drinking. Granting us a pass to make total fools of ourselves on the dance floor as no one would suspect that we were totally sober as we embraced life and the music. I would lose myself within each song as it created the perfect space for my soul to heal as the pounding base vibrated through my body.

I twirled and twisted my body letting my arms and hands flow wherever they desired watching them glide back and forth. It was as if pure energy was flowing right out of my very fingertips painting the room as it created a technicolour work of art.

I spun around catching a glimpse of my girlfriend who was now grinning her usual beautiful smile as she stretched out her finger pointing to grab my attention. Turning to see what spectacle was of so much interest I saw *him*. He was tall, and handsome with short dark hair. He had a skater-boy look to him as he coasted across the dance floor in his converse kicks and NOFX T-shirt. I had seen many good-looking guys during our outings, but this time was different. Different because for some reason I stopped dancing and just observed him. Despite him not being my usual type there was something about him that was so familiar and so calm all I could do was stand there and stare.

Before I could come up with a rapid-fire, 'No, I don't like…' I paused.

Then hearing the very word 'maybe' make its way from my lips shocking even myself in disbelief. My girlfriend's eyes almost popped out of her head as she instantly shoved me towards him, damn near knocking me off my own feet.

There was something different about him, but what? After a quick introduction. "Hi, I'm Jen," I nervously hear the words rumble from my mouth. Suddenly feeling the oddness of me approaching him. He sheepishly told me his name was 'Kevin'. We barely talked but we continued to dance away that magical night. Throughout the rest of the evening, I could feel my little spark light up with each song. As the night ended, he offered to walk me home. My girlfriend jumped at this opportunity to leave early, however, not before she said to text her when I got home to make sure he was not a stalker.

As we left the pub, we soon discovered we both lived on the same street two city blocks away from each other. So weird. Laughing now as I write this knowing full well that the Universe had a master plan for me.

And the rest as they say is history. Well sort of, it may have taken me moving back home to repair my relationship with my parents in order for me not to rush into another relationship. Then having my father of all people plant a seed in my mind that Kevin may indeed be a keeper.

We got married and lived happily ever after is how I like to recall these years.

Confirming that even after thirteen years I can safely say he is a 'keeper' but like most couples who find themselves on the other end of the honeymoon sensing the stress of work, career changes, moving four times across three provinces and two kids could be felt. Once again, I found myself still searching for my spark. More than not laying in my bed at night wondering how everyone else was doing. My husband, my two kids, even the health of my dogs before asking myself how are you? Really how are you? What are you feeling? Did you enjoy your day?

I yearned to feel that incredible spark of connection. Only instead of finding a lasting spark of hope I felt the sadness pulling me back down into the abyss of feeling lost. Lost as to what and where to start. Questioning everything.

What did I need? A purpose? A new mindset? Maybe that was the answer. A new mindset to help guide me forward to my true purpose of self-love and self-growth.

As I went searching for my purpose a flame or at least a spark of positive energy and perseverance would ignite. A flame of joy and love to feel more and do more. Calling to me like never before creating this fiery energy driving me to accomplish many amazing things that I would have thought in the past were impossible things.

The more I looked into how I could feed this spark's fiery energy it brought into question my current mindset, brain power and potential. After all, 'they say', we only use ten percent of our brain's energy or true potential. Joking aside, this may be Hollywood's favourite pseudoscience stat that human beings only use ten percent of their brain power; however, I am a true believer in this untapped resource. A resource that I relished in the idea that I still have all this potential and room to grow unlocking the key to my own matrix.

I had heard of this statistic before but never really thought of how it applied to me personally, especially to my own potential. Curiosity began to fuel my fire as I began to understand and refuse to believe that my potential is limited.

Seriously, what is that other ninety percent potential power used for? What exactly does energy do and how can I make more of it?

As I worked on opening my mind up to my true potential, I could sense a spark within. You, crazy little spark who are you? What are you? Why and how for all these years was I so drawn to you? What fuelled you? What gave you energy? What gave *me* energy to grow?

After all, it is the one and only factor that gave me relief from all this sadness. Energetic spark with your unconditional gentle voice calling me back no matter how many times I needed it. Possessing a golden profound sense of awe of being home or in the exact right place at the right time. No matter where I was in life it was always there for me. I could not possibly be the only one who feels this need to find you.

The acknowledgement that I was somehow only utilising that ten percent of my true potential left me to wonder. Wondering how on earth I could access that other ninety percent? As I reflected back upon that inspiring morning back in college that sparked my inner 'Wonder Women' to adorn her cape and rise up as she taped into that illusive, ninety percent, in order to live and fight another day.

Seriously, what was this spark I felt? As apparently a spark is a small fiery particle thrown off from a fire, alight in ashes, or produced by striking together two hard surfaces such as stone or metal as loosely explained by the Oxford dictionary.

'By striking together two hard surfaces', much like life in all its glory can also be full of friction and heated uncomfortable situations.

'Alight in ashes', as one may find themselves after said situation buried in that pile of ashes as the smoke clears in search for that small spark or light at the end of a difficult dark tunnel.

One thing was for sure, there was an energetic power in that incredible fiery spark.

Sometimes, I saw rare glimpses of the red-hot flames. If I managed to stand strong, breathe and open my mind up to gratitude and just watch the flame it would grow even more. Feeding it with each grateful breath releasing and increasing the size of the flame. Even after it went out this spark always left me wanting more.

Noticing that if I let in self-doubt the spark would go out. If I let in sadness the spark would go out. Leaving me to wallow in my own self-pity.

Spark is such an accurate depiction of my journey of continual self-growth. As inspiration guides me in and out of situations. I began to understand that the inspiration of that spark is found where the *dark + light* meet where it resided flourishing in the vast empty space between the two.

To understand this spark, I had to delve deeper into my understanding of energy. Even in grade school we were taught that molecules contain ninety-nine percent of empty space.

However, even according to an article in Forbes magazine: "You are not mostly empty space." If you were to look at what your body is made of, at smaller and more fundamental levels, you'd find a whole miniature Universe of structure inside you:

https://www.forbes.com/sites/startswithabang/2020/0 4/16/you-are-not-mostly-empty-space/?sh=3dbb3be22c2b

As to not lose you in scientific facts, my layman's knowledge is that: Empty space found within our molecules was once thought as actual empty space containing nothing but is now known as dark matter or energy. Which I thought was incredibly interesting due to the fact that if you were to remove all of the empty space contained in every atom in every person on planet earth and compress us all together as one, then the overall volume of our particles would be smaller than a sugar cube. Proving once again the importance of energy versus our physical bodies.

As my understanding and purpose of energy for this beautiful spark became clearer. This clarity forged between energy and spark created a bonded connection to what I call 'Universe'. Also known as God, Buddha, Jesus, Gaia, Mother Earth, Akasha, One, Universal Energy, Seed, Source, or nothing in particular.

It really does not matter what name you give it. It is all the same, it is the one thing that helps drive us to be the best versions of ourselves. It is the one life-giving creative force. Along my journey, I found that the name 'Universe' resonated for me. A Universe which is a vast all-encompassing oneness, the no one excluded oneness, the no one above or below oneness, the pure infinite unconditional positive spark of energy oneness.

A universal energy which is fuelled by our emotions, thoughts, words, and actions. Constantly being fed by two types of forces, positive and negative energy. Positive energy that has the ability to create evolutionary growth and negative energy that has the power to destroy the process of creativity. Both of these have the power to greatly change one's path as they contain an equal value and need. Positive and negative energy are ruled by a scientific law known to us as the 'Law of Attraction'. You may or may not have heard of this law or ever thought of how it pertains to your daily life. I admit I had never used it to guide me. More so referring to it as a product of circumstances or outcomes.

In all the nothingness and sadness, a new hope for creating something more for myself emerged. But what? I have so many questions to work through. How the heck does one go about feeding their spirit with this energy? Am I creating it?

As I delve into energy, I have come to a confident and comfortable place around energy that made sense to me. Being a visual learner with a desire to keep this concept of energy realistic, relatable, and simple for myself. Remembering that each of you will have your own names, concepts and visualisations which will resonate differently and uniquely to your own personal experiences.

As I continue sharing my journey, I would like to take a breath to set an intention to create a spark from within you or maybe even evoke a present one to burn a little brighter.

"Your spirit is the part of you that feels like hope." — Carolyn Myss.

I love to imagine energy as a ball of light packed full of love and hope. A fiery ball that has the ability to guide me in a positive way. A tiny spark leads the way fuelling itself off positive emotions, thoughts, words, and actions. Imagining that the golden energy is sparked by unconditional love. The energy which can serve up a juicy meal for my spirit. A satisfying meal of unconditional love that had the potential to evolve personal growth as I felt it rising in my chest or tingles up my spine as it floods through the rest of my body.

Other times when it was gone it was just a heavy black feeling. A feeling of being alone, sad and disconnected. No spark, no light, just blackness. I wondered: does this mean something was wrong with me? Am I broken?

Relentlessly doubting myself, only to ultimately reassure myself that it just meant that I was human. This detached state of starving my spirit had the ability to make one feel broken, relishing in a constant state of lack. However, once I acknowledged that I had never lost or broken my connection, I had just forgotten how to use it as the relief sets back in.

You may be tapping into your own spark right now or you may be rolling your eyes. No worries, I am not here to tell you what you should or should not believe in. I am here to speak my truth of personal growth. A personal growth journey in search of releasing this gripping sadness, as I document and share my evolution over the next three hundred and sixty-five days. Nor is this book about the perfect plan or a perfect formula to discover self-love. This is a book of evidence that each person has their own path of self-love and awareness. A path that can be an extremely messy and turbulent yet amazing and rewarding all wrapped up into one journey.

My only advice is to be patient and open. Open to receiving, learning, giving yourself time and unconditional love to apply the good that comes along your path. With a set intention to spread positive inspiration and energy with each word shared.

Some of my greatest revelations and ah-ha moments were from hearing of other people's personal journeys, which is why I felt so compelled to document and share my own journey with you. I invite you to join me in sitting down to a juicy meal of inspiration and hope.

CHAPTER 3

No time, except for excuses

As I relished in the bliss of yesterday's spark, finding myself trying to formulate a plan of action for healing. It fuelled my spirit with the prospect of creating more for myself but quickly shifted to a turbulent state of overwhelmed emotions as feelings of disconnection settled in.

With so many excuses, and so little time. Sadness and doubt started to pull me under, sounding the alarms that this ship was going to sink. *Beep. Beep. Beep.* Echoing a negative constant warning of signal as to why there simply was not enough. Not enough information. Not enough knowledge on this subject of healing. Not enough love, enough patience, enough energy, even my day never seemed to be long enough.

Who was I to think I could heal myself?

Seriously, why start something you could not possibly accomplish? These tsunami size excuses started to build into a massive wave of doubt within me. As one final debilitating breaking wave with its extreme power plunged me into the depths as I smashed into the rocks below its surface.

Ultimately rendering me helpless and face down in the foetal position on my couch as I lay there not wanting to move. After all, I have a whole year to figure this out. What is the rush? Instead of pushing through these excuses and swimming my way to the surface. I decided it was easier to just do nothing. Easier to just lay here scrolling through my Facebook feed while I watched Netflix and chill.

As drowning perfectly depicts my state of mind over the last few days of being restricted by negative excuses. Making movement nearly impossible to flow towards anything positive.

As the salty excuses blur my vision with sadness, fear, and anxiety my mind reminded me that this was a familiar comfortable place. Reinforcing my mind's conditioned state for avoiding friction at all costs. Even at the cost of my own life. It seemed as if it was easier to do nothing than challenge myself to do more or specifically to be more.

After many days I finally admitted to myself that I had an incessant need to give in to these negative feelings. Awareness that I felt the friction does not mean I had to take it all in and gulp it down. Casting a light on having the ability to acknowledge friction's emotional ties to overwhelming senses of sorrow, anger, stress, and guilt without the simple fact of fuelling it.

I knew in my heart that my personal growth hinged on the ability to face the friction. What if I could find a way of pushing off from the depths to save myself for once? Would that fire up my spark? If not, I knew I would only find excuses. My choice was to simply swim or die a slow death of sadness.

Awakening in that one single moment to no longer be fooled into the familiar lull of this wave. Seeing right through the negative energy and finally admitting to myself that I was *not* avoiding the wave of friction. I was simply gulping it down, giving my thoughts permission to drown me.

Step one would be to acknowledge that in thinking I was avoiding friction at all costs inevitably drown me. Drown me with all these suppressed emotions and negative self-talk. Granting friction permission to toss my spirit around like a rag doll in a washing machine removing all self-worth.

Step two would be to observe this behaviour. I was flabbergasted at the sheer number of times I never stood up for myself in order to avoid friction. So much so that I started to record it all down in a journal. Not all friction needs an exchange of actions or words. However, smiling and acting like I agreed in order to avoid the friction of conflict seemed to be killing me slowly from the inside out manifesting itself as health issues.

I began acknowledging friction as I recorded these events down on paper. This seems to be an incredible tool in granting me a voice to heal and grow. I quickly recognized that my journaling was taking on a life of its own, inspiring me to be more accountable for each day. As I began to understand that everything does happen at the perfect time for the perfect reason, I reassured myself that the more I connect with my mind, my body, and my spirit the quicker the spark could be felt. I started to feel a fusion of all my lost pieces the more I began to genuinely see myself for where I currently existed.

Morphing itself into a story of how I found my spark and became alive. A miracle not unlike Pinocchio as he transformed from a wood carved puppet to a real-life boy.

You may be thinking but I hate writing or journaling, it is not for me. Frankly, I would have agreed and said you were bat-shit crazy if you thought I would journal about myself. Much less write about any of my life, experiences, or feelings. Especially after spending the better part of my thirties picking my way through all the lice-filled events. Seriously, I had finally recovered from my past and was now determined to live a more abundant life. Fully committed to living by one simple motto. 'What is in the past, can stay in the past'.

Just the thought of dredging everything back up, recording it, and sharing this journey would have sent me tumbling down a black hole of denial. However, the power in recording these simple acts of avoiding friction became abundantly clear that it did indeed awaken my elusive spark.

A clear comprehension that to profoundly move on and concur this sadness things inevitably had to get uncomfortable. I would need to push myself to do things I never thought were possible such as body surfing a tsunami wave naked. Even if it meant getting down to the nitty-gritty of removing all the layers as I stripped myself down to the most vulnerable state.

With this simple decision to acknowledge friction, I began journaling my emotional behaviours. Emotions that brought about many 'holy crap this is working moments'. Moments that allowed me to see past these waves which came hand in hand with excuses for what they genuinely were. Just that waves. Waves that would come and go, often just as quickly as they presented themselves. Some are much bigger than others but it's not the end of the world as I knew it.

Embracing this sensation of no longer avoiding friction allowed me to harness its power. A power that carried me to the possibility of true safety. With this newfound power, I felt my spark explode into a fiery ball as my heart vibrated and my body relaxed into weightlessness. It was as if the wave of the water cradled my body bringing me back up to its surface and allowed the warm sun to kiss my face.

Even now, a tingling wave of energy rushes up my spine as I recall this fiery inspiration of stripping friction of its power bringing with it feelings of gratitude as it filled up my very being.

Thank you! Thank you, sweet baby Jesus. Thank you, Universe.

The creative process of writing in any form whether it be poetry, journaling, documenting, or song writing can be one of the most therapeutic, moving, and evolving experiences. Believe me when I say that I used to be a person who knew the power of writing but rarely if ever embraced it. I was more of a talker than a note taker admitting that the challenge of documenting one's emotional struggles and triumphs is a story all in itself. Noting that as I slugged through all the emotions as they arise it seems to challenge me on the best of days. A challenge that reminds me of just how human we all are and how powerful our words can be.

Therefore, if you think I just sat down over the year pouring my heart into working on personal growth and documenting this journey as an effortless stream of wisdom and revelations that would be the furthest thing from the truth. Most days it was jarring, slow, painful, and even terrifying yet as the days passed more than not it became an exhilarating journey accompanied by countless tears of sorrow but even more tears of revelations and growth.

Reminding myself that the key to growth was acknowledging everything comes from within. The good, the bad and sometimes even the ugly all have their own purpose. Even my excuses had a purpose.

With time and gentle coxing, I saw the value and purpose that these excuses possessed as I incessantly began recording and working through them. Knowing full well there will be an excuse to be found if I look long and hard enough. I confess that I may very well have traded my addiction to alcohol for an addiction to excuses.

Coming to terms with the fact that I was avoiding friction at all costs in order to feed my addiction to excuses rendered me the excuse addict that I was. An addict who got off on excuses and who seemed more content with the uncomfortable chaos of the waves drowning me as I refused the help of the universal flow to safely carry me to the surface.

Finally understanding the value in just admitting this action stripped away the power from all these excuses. In turn, releasing the need to fight against the current. I could feel a sense of healing wash over me. It was as if I could finally breathe in the clean crisp air. Finding that the key to riding this daunting wave was to simply accept that it was present as I breathed in new ideas for a solution. On a good day, it even resulted in a positive mindset allowing me to see the positive side of the negative situation as I worked my way to becoming a problem solver instead of a problem maker.

With 345 days left, I began to observe and record my behaviour without judgement or expectation. Every once in a while, I would check in to keep myself accountable and release any preconceived ideas of guilt. I soon realised just how aggressive and sometimes uncomfortable it must be to watch me. Some days I am sure I mirrored a shark sinking to the depths of the ocean as I devoured my prey, ripping it into shreds leaving it in pieces. Allowing my mood-induced excuses to take over. The best days at hand were when I could observe myself as a beautiful swan floating through my day with ease and grace on the calm, cool water's surface. OK, maybe more like mimicking a Canada Goose but joking aside, an obvious change could be seen.

Observing my behaviour and taking mental notes for the day was a good start. However, the real change came when the mental notetaking became a to-do list. Learning from previous trials that mental note-taking is all well and good, but an action list is what gets shit done. So, I set out to record what I observed throughout the day without judgement.

These notes became my sort of to-do list. Aiding me in releasing this underlying sadness and reminding myself of the importance to keep this list short and manageable. As I stepped back and observed without judgement, this list would change, evolve, and grow throughout my year of healing. A list which turned into an invaluable tool of observation which I still use to this day.

To do list:
_ be aware of friction and excuses
_ be present
_ take time for myself

_ quick negative reactions and thoughts — why? fix attitude

_ work on fear, reset my mindset.

These were just a few of my tasks as the list evolved. With a need to start small and focus on one to-do task at a time. Being present seemed like a good place to start or as Wayne Dyer had perfectly put it, "Be Here Now".

Trying to bring my focus to the present moment by slowing down allows me to come into the present moment. A moment not of the past or the future but right here, right now. Be and feel in this very moment as I observed all the sights, sounds, smells, and the emotions around me without judgement.

This movement to become present is new to me as my mind currently is at warp speed constantly time travelling from the past to the future and finally but rarely landing on the present. Constantly consumed with all the tasks that demanded to be done. I silently watched how I carried out my day, noting to myself that my present mind is extremely distracted while speaking or listening to others.

This morning was a prime example of where my present state of my mind was at. My son, Spencer, rushed up the stairs feverishly explaining to me all the particulars of his thrilling new game. Giving me an incredibly detailed and colourful explanation of the exceptionally rare character, he had just earned. Going into great detail about how hard he had worked in order to master these new fighting skills to acquire such an amazing character.

I found myself staring at his face blankly. Any human could have felt his rush of excitement yet while he spoke, all I could think of was 'hurry up! I need to get ready for work because I have so many important pressing tasks to get done this morning'. Tasks that I meticulously noted and reviewed in my mind as he spoke. Resulting in me giving him a 'good job' and flashing a quick fake smile as I interrupt the storytelling bringing all to an abrupt end. Only to have him walk away looking disappointed at my lack of attention and enthusiasm.

As he walked away, my eyes followed his path leaving me with no actual recollection of what he had just said. Instead permitting a steady flow of negative excuses to flood into my mind. He is young and just doesn't understand how important my job is. Frankly, I just don't have time for this.

Now fully aware of this moment, I stop. I take in a deep breath.

I quickly realise just how ridiculous these excuses are as I try to bring my mind back to the present moment. Admitting to myself that I was not paying any respect or attention to his words or the positive energy that he was so eagerly trying to share with me. Vowing to myself that the next time he spoke to me I would unquestionably try to '*be here now*'.

As I struggle to stay in the present moment the questions start to flood in. Why was this happening? Why was work more important and more valued? This awareness that I only feel successful and valued if I am busy starts to set in. Relentlessly basing my success of the day on how well and just how many tasks were completed. With little to no attention or value put on the relationships with others that crossed my path as the day unfolded and tasks completed.

The smiles never counted, laughs never counted, sunsets watched never counted even the heartfelt conversations never counted. For a person who had prided herself on 'my job is just what I do, it is not who I am'. Why did I grant my mind and tasks so much power? Currently, my mind is running the show and calling all the shots fully sensing once again that there was a serious disconnection with my mind, body, and spirit.

'*Breathe*'.

As I take in another deep breath, I repeat my mantra to just observe not to judge but to learn and implement.

Instead of giving into past conditioning of spiralling into guilt with feelings of being a failure as a parent, I jump at the opportunity to implement change. I then make my way downstairs to give Spencer a huge hug and apologise to him that I am truly sorry that I was not listening and to please repeat his story if he so desires.

My heart fills with warmth as I watch his energy shift. With each word, his eyes light up in delight. The guilt over the previous conversation quickly vanishes along with the pressure to do more and be more. Alleviating this self-imposed pressure to be the perfect parent who needed to be busy every moment of the day. This made way for a noticeable shift within both of our spirits as we started to feel the exchange of positive energy and a beautiful smile made its way across his face. Shifting my attention to a more important job. A job of being present in my new career with one mission in life which was to embrace this precious conversation while my son spoke.

"You cannot nor need to fix yourself.

Instead, just be and live as the person you want you to be." — quote by Abraham Hicks.

As I reflect on this quote, I remind myself that written words have the power to evoke positive change but only if implemented. I began reminiscing over the emotional charge that this quote had evoked in me as I had taken this initial screenshot on my social media account. Now finding myself laughing at the realisation of the sheer number of saved inspirational screenshots currently bombarding my phone.

The universe has a funny way of presenting the most crucial tools of life that are needed in order to grow and evolve. A universe that had its work cut out for itself as it usually took, presenting me numerous times with multiple inspirations of hope to spark positive change.

Leaving me to question what my motives were and what I planned on doing with all these inspirational screenshots on my phone. Apparently, it was just to use up all my phone's memory, never to be implemented into daily practice only later to be mass deleted.

At that moment I realised that I tended to spend more time on my phone in the evening when things slowed down, scrolling on my social feed to avoid dealing with feelings of boredom or sadness. Snapping these inspirational quotes to provide myself with a quick dose of momentary happiness. Funny, the universe was practically yelling at me if only I would listen and implement what it was trying to teach me.

Confirming that the one and only true lasting change I can make in my lifetime is the change I make for myself. With this understanding, I accept my role with the universe to be present as I implement these inspirational tools.

Reality check-in

Mind check-in:

Riding the rollercoaster of my daily excuses.

Body check-in:

Getting up thirty minutes earlier but still not excited to get up even after four to five snoozes. Feeling frustrated.

Spirit check-in:

Currently fluctuating on a continual sliding scale from spiritual connection to a tragic drowning.

Friction is described as being the force between two solid surfaces as they 'chafe against each other in a forceful way' much like life. Making my way through difficult situations and events could also be described in this manner. The uncomfortable feeling when people piss me off or a situation that does not go my way. Amplified when something disappoints me, something breaks, or people get sick and die the list goes on and on, but I think you get the idea.

Funny how easily I can relate to all the feelings associated with friction describing them to a tee but spark on the other hand seemed to be a foreign concept to explain, feel and create at times. This place of friction for me was not a happy place which as you know I avoided like the plague. Finding myself even now that I am now fully aware of its purpose to teach and guide me, I am left wondering how and why shitty circumstances are still happening to me?

Constantly living in my bubble of protection trying to keep anything negative and everyone that was not aligned with my current mindset out. Little did I realise that when that phone rang this evening that the universe was going to imprint a blessing of the true purpose of friction into my very being.

What started off as a normal everyday phone conversation with a friend ended in her saying something so hurtful and so profound it changed the way I look at friction and myself forever. As I explained to her how I was currently struggling working through letting go of all the excuses I had grown so fond of.

She then proceeded to interrupt me with one simple statement *'Stop feeling so sorry for yourself'*. What the fuck was my first, second and third thought as her words blasted through my mind and body.

I could feel my face become red hot as the anger surfaced, but still I said nothing only to quickly retreat and make up some lame excuse as to why it was necessary to immediately hang up the phone. Leaving me dumbfounded as to how someone could be so inconsiderate, thoughtless, and cruel all at the same time considering all I had been through and how far I had come.

Believe me, growing up with an alcoholic had its challenges as rude comments thicken my skin against such verbal attacks but somehow this was different. It was so unexpected as this insult was coming from a friend who had grown near and dear to me. Continual thoughts rampaged my mind on repeat. Thoughts that I most definitely do not feel sorry for myself. Honestly, I am the most selfless person I know. Totally pissed off and consumed by this hurtful and ridiculous statement I proceeded to tell my husband Kevin about this heinous crime just committed against me as the tears welled in my eyes. He could clearly see my pain as I reiterated her mean-spirited words, yet he said little to nothing. Simply giving me a huge hug and reassuring me that I would work it all out which left me thoroughly irritated with his lack of sympathy. This only added fuel to my anger. I then headed off to bed early, still fuming.

Day after day that hurtful little statement resurfaced. Stuck on repeat, it taunted me.

'Stop feeling so sorry for yourself'.

As my anger and betrayal increased with even more voracity. After about a week of this anger, my mind was now exhausted from being drained of energy by this statement and countless hours spent mulling over the conversation that we had.

I had had enough.

Enough of the incessant walking around in a storm of anger not sleeping compounded by being totally consumed by this comment, I decided to turn to a little therapeutic baking. Also known as eating so I could stuff my face with chocolate chip cookies and lick my wounds. As the mixer whipped all the ingredients together, I stared hypnotically at the swirling beaters as it whisked the batter around and around lulling me into a relaxed state.

'*Breathe*'.

Zoning out I seemed to have allowed my body and mind to go quiet. I recall taking in that deep breath and then letting it go as a foreign-sounding sigh made its way to the surface. A gentle and loving voice popped into my heart. "Do I feel sorry for myself?" I had an epiphany, 'H.H.H.O.L.L.L.Y *shit*! *I do feel sorry for myself*. In fact, a whole week of not sleeping, bitching, and complaining not feeling sorry for myself to be exact.

Tears of relief started to stream down my face the instant I had acknowledged these emotions. Emotions which required space to be expressed. Space that allowed a release of pity, stress and anger to be felt followed by a release as it flowed out from my body allowing me to make my way back to the surface. What just happened, this strange and glorious feeling?

I quickly became aware that I could not waste this 'holy shit' moment by going back to my pity party as it was clearly life-changing. In a state of my ugly cry, I dialled up that friend to share just how profound this revelation had shifted my mindset. A shift that now allowed me to thank her as we both proceeded to shed a few tears over personal growth and just how human we all are.

This was the fiction I needed in order to grow. The kind of friction that saw the importance in observing our own behaviour without judgement. Once again proving that friction is a powerful tool. A tool to see the importance of releasing a need to be a people pleaser and that by expressing myself in that present moment could be the key to less suffering and limitless growth.

Reality check-in

Mind check-in:

Feeling slightly less stubborn and more open.

Body check-in:

Energised for one moment. Exhausted the next. Blah.

Spirit check-in:

Connected. Not connected. Connected. Not connected.

Doubt and fear came hand in hand with this newfound awareness that I was feeling sorry for myself. Trying to reassure myself was scary as hell because if I did *not* feel sorry for myself any more, what would I *feel*?

Would old emotions of guilt, anger, and resentment return? It would be so much easier to slip back into my little pity party, that I had so meticulously created and toiled with over the years. In spite of the discomfort, something was pushing me to do more and to be more. To challenge myself and to feel that I was worth the upgrade of replacing pity with another emotion, especially a positive one.

I thought, why not just choose to be happy and not a self-pitying victim?

I have heard this statement a million times: that 'Happiness is a Choice'.

Even so until today I never fully understood or felt it. However, this time it was vastly different. This was a moment of devotion to myself, that I was worthy of being happy. Genuinely happy. Not putting on a fake smile while feeling horrible inside, happy. The real deal. For once I felt a spark of sheer joy that I had the confidence to choose happiness for myself.

This ah-ha moment began to open my mind, setting me on a mission to see how many more of these moments I could apply to myself. This was definitely the wake-up call I desired as the flow of constant growth and resets carried me along. Strengthening the emotional tether of my spirit to this flow. I became hyper aware of when I was happy and sad, constantly trying to check in with myself to assess my emotions, thoughts, actions and especially my reactions. Most days what used to take me weeks to turn excuses and self-pity into positive thoughts, now presented themselves much more rapidly and effortlessly as the solution unfolded.

Inspired to leave a lasting imprint I noted in my journal in big bold letters, 'FRICTION IS A TOOL'.

Therefore, in order for me to implement what I have learned I would need to acknowledge the situation. Not what I perceived as happening but what was truly happening. Most times my mind and emotions had blown the event out of proportion. Creating a much more turbulent outcome than the situation warranted as I noted the pain and suffering, I had created for myself.

And so began the work of trying to stay afloat. The more I resisted the friction with an instant '*No*. Not me. Not happening'. An alarm would be triggered within me. Almost akin to an instant SOS call warning of hazards which if ignored would cause a catastrophic sinking.

Breathe, I remind myself. You got this.

More than not, attempting to address these alarms also triggered unwarranted emotional eruptions. However, understanding that I was like a child just learning how to express oneself gracefully for the first time was the key. An understanding that would take time and patience to master. Finally confirming as I released judgement that I was indeed on a journey of healing.

CHAPTER 4

Fixing my shitty attitude

Announcing her royal highness, red carpet, and all. My shitty attitude appeared to be larger than life acting as though she was a Hollywood movie star. She is strutting her stuff on that plush carpet for all to adore. Creating a spectacle so that everyone around noticed her presence as she worked the room. Magically appearing when life became challenging.

This morning was not unlike most mornings, for example, her heels fully dug into the luxurious plush red carpet as she appeared to be spouting on about not being able to find something. Something so special and precious that was more important than the happiness or feelings of her family.

Her earbuds, her precious, precious earbuds! Obviously, someone must have taken them. Triggering her Royal Highness to display a raging hissy fit as she tears through the house frantically searching for her precious. All the while slamming drawers and stomping up and down the stairs. She was royally pissed off. Demanding that, 'Everyone is always taking my stuff, and no one ever puts anything back!' Then followed by a few choice words mumbled under her breath but still loud enough for all to hear. 'Fine, don't help me!'

Her Royal Highness then retreats to her bedroom to cool off. Rounding the corner, she sees her beloved earbuds sitting on her nightstand right where she left them the day before. Oops! Apparently, no apologies are necessary. Nothing, not even a word, just continuing on her royal day as if nothing has transpired.

Viciously grabbing the earbuds off the nightstand, she anxiously spins around to make sure no one has caught sight of this mishap but rather manages to connect eye to eye with herself in the bedroom mirror.

"*Shit*," I gasp.

I almost didn't recognize my own face as my eyes blazed in sheer anger. '*Breathe*'.

The air enters my lungs as my attention now shifts to my reddened cheeks which are royally flushed with embarrassment. One thing was for sure I did not like what I saw. An overreacting, blaming, verbally assaulting, and out of control being. Frankly, she was a royal bitch.

'*Breathe*'.

The guilt that transpired from the way I spoke and acted around my family was now compounded by the guilt of the lost earbuds being solely my fault. This was another one of those unexpected 'holy crap moments'. I quickly added this to my to-do list acknowledging that just because I am aware of my shitty attitude did not fix it.

I could be a royal bitch and I finally understood the importance of claiming this title. Fixing my shitty attitude would take a full-sized Hollywood blacklisting. As most people around me would say I had an incredibly positive 'go get am' attitude as a person who always looked on the bright side.

Absolutely. I did appear like I had my life all figured out as I was at peace with the flow of life and everything happening around me. But honestly down deep especially when things slowed down my life was anything, but Zen. In the quiet safety of my home, chilling her royal highness of shitty attitudes would appear frequently in full force. As today's typical ordeal unfolded, I recognized my pattern of working hard to maintain my composure, patience, and a loving persona only to arrive home with little to no composure, patience, understanding, or love left for my own family.

Exhausted by these feelings of living a lie that seemed to drain what little energy I had left. Feelings that left nothing for those closest to me. A drain of energy which nonetheless still had the ability to strangely fuel overwhelming sadness towards others but mainly towards myself. Utterly exhausted by my emotions of feeling as if I had lost something I never knew I had. Months later, I will come to the realisation that I did lose something — my ability to love and believe in myself.

"Your life is a result of the choices you make...

If you do not like your life, it is time to start making better choices." — Unknown.

Confessing that I had a shitty attitude was pivotal to blacklisting her royal highness for once and for all. Continually taking baby steps to not judge myself and to just observe that my attitude had a hand in everything I did right down to my everyday reactions. Regarding the way I viewed myself and others especially when it came to parenting and interacting with my husband and kids.

This shitty attitude seemed so familiar to me. So familiar it was scary as if it was the only concept of dealing with issues that I had in the safety of my home. Understanding without judgement that this indeed was my only natural go-to for blowing off steam that had built up throughout the day. My only technique was to embrace her royal highness as she rampaged at home. After all, I needed to put on a good show when I was out, much like the movie.

So why did these outbursts feel so familiar? Even comfortable for all of these years? I became abruptly aware that my parenting coping traits were echoing those I had been conditioned to growing up. This was a serious slap in the face as a wake-up call to reality. The reality I dreaded the most, parenting like my parents. Like most children growing up I always told myself I would never parent like my parents. Only to discover now as a parent that my current parenting style echoed that of my parent's parenting, now adopting this as my own style. The act of putting on a big show in order to be taken seriously. As memories of my father feeling a need to stream out his demands, rehashing them for hours to make his point and claim his role.

Do not get me wrong there were good parts of their parenting style that I valued growing up. Such as giving and helping others. An amazing generosity of giving the shirt off your back if someone required it. The kind of generosity that even my ten-year-old self had acknowledged was of value as a parenting trait.

But like most things in life, my focus on the negative outweighed the positive. Another wonderful attribute of my shitty attitude which was extremely hard to acknowledge but was essential to furthering my own personal growth. If I truly desired growth, I would need to just accept this realisation. A realisation that I too had continued this cycle of a shitty attitude as a person who treated everyone else with more importance and value than those closest to me. Sharing and saving my best behaviour for everyone else other than my own family. The best laughs, best parts of my patience, and best efforts to be more.

This awareness was difficult but essential to addressing my shitty attitude. I became overtly aware that her royal highness was currently wrapped so tightly in excuses and conditioning that it reinforced this negative behaviour. How could one not see these excuses now that I was aware of them as each new circumstance arose as I accepted the need for change. I try to convince myself that this is an easy fix. A fix that only takes making a different choice of how to react and interact with those closest to me.

'I can do this; I can choose. All I had to do was choose to be loving and patient'. At least that is what I told myself. However, what I wanted for myself and what I was currently capable of doing were two vastly different things. Baby steps I remind myself, do not judge, just observe.

The more I just sat in my parenting and homelife analysis, the more I comprehended that my royal highness's attitude had lightning-fast reflexes. Supersonic to be exact with the ability to crush anyone in her way with one foul step of her high heel. As she trampled any innocent bystanders face down into that red carpet with little to no consideration for anyone in her path. Regardless of which family member you were or where you were. My reaction time between the current circumstance at hand and my verbal reaction was so rapid and sharp. Shocking even myself as it zipped right through me at breakneck speeds. Instantly reacting, as if my life depended on that one quick swift blow of a reaction with virtually no time to formulate a loving answer in any sort of rational, thoughtful, or calm reply.

Who has time to make a positive choice with that lightning-fast reaction rate? Definitely not me, not yet.

Reality check-in.

Mind check-in:

Aware of needing to break this cycle of being me — so frustrating.

Body check-in:

Trying to motivate myself to make more healthy choices to eat better and exercise more.

Spiritual check-in:

I find myself lost in pep talks of disconnect and connected as I limbo back and forth.

As I venture down the path to addressing my shitty attitude, I find myself reading, listening, and watching many resources which all seem to talk about breathing. Learning to breathe is something I thought of as automatic as the very term breath is to take air into the lungs and then expel it, as a regular physiological process.

This pretty much sums up how I have survived on autopilot breathing my way through life with little to no acknowledgement of inhalation and exhalation's vast importance or true potential. Never utilising it as an actual tool for growth and healing only to learn that there was so much more to the breath. How to breathe? How long to breathe? How to hold my breath? How to use my breath to heal? How to use my breath to reset my body? How to use my breath to release stress and anxiety? How to use my breath to create space?

Yes, the autopilot breathing part I had down pat without thinking or any effort necessary on my behalf. Sure, I did yoga over the years with breathwork playing an integral part, but I still seemed to look at it in its simplest form as just a way to regulate my body during the workout. Controlling my breath in order to workout harder, faster, and stronger. Never about strengthening my connection to the universe, nor will my own spirit and definitely not using it daily for personal growth and healing.

The science behind the breath and how it helps generate energy, connection, life, and stability in the body is something altogether new to me. There were so many different types of breathing methods that one could explore. Some I have loved some I hated, and some I still desired to master as I began to integrate mindful breathing into my day. However, I still found that I limited its use to being my go-to only when I was utterly stressed out. Regardless, this would be a great start as quick cleansing breaths instantly gave me relief. Almost like a magical pill that when taken instantly increased my energy flow and cleared my mind when dealing with stressful situations.

"Just breathe motherfucker."

— Wim Hof

I couldn't agree more with Mr Hof. Wim is a Dutch extreme athlete who swears that cold therapy can be a powerful tool for the immune system and regulating one's stress response.

Reminding myself to just breathe as I thanked the universe once again for crossing my path with such an inspirational man as I uploaded my new screensaver smiling at the colourful words 'just breathe, motherfucker'.

This would become the perfect reminder to embrace my breath, not to react, but to just breathe. Especially in those heated moments when stress and anger wanted to rage. I began to implement and experience the energy of my breath within each emotional wave of pure energy as the warmth began to wash over me. Sensing the energy take on a life of its own as if time itself was bending in order to create a space with the sole purpose of filling me with peace and reassurance of connection. The tears began to flow down my face as I allowed this breath into my body embracing its full effect on my soul. I acknowledged that in the past my conditioning of suppressing these unknown emotions was indeed happening numerous times a day.

This breath would now allow me to deal considerably much more effectively with her Royal Highness. Even as I felt her presence screaming within me demanding her needs, I just breathed and observed. I will no longer be fooled by past conditioning for rapid negative reactions intertwined with the pressure of her heels digging into that red carpet.

Fully aware of this newfound essential need to just stop, stop right here and take a simple cleansing breath. Reminding myself that life is fleeting and that I, myself was speeding up what precious little time that I did have. Confessing if I was speeding time up, it also meant that I too had the ability to slow it down resulting in the creation of more time and space. Harnessing the potential of this process would take time, but with genuine effort would ultimately have the ability to change my life and how I reacted to confrontation and difficult situations.

Reality check-in

Mind check-in:

Trying to slow things down as I sense that my life is a constant grind of wake up, work, eat, chill, sleep, repeat only to yearn for weekends and days off. I want happiness now, not later, not tomorrow, or next year.

Body check-in:

Set a new goal of getting up early to give myself more time as I continue to struggle with needing just one more snooze.

Spiritual check-in:

Being present and open to change I started repeating this little affirmation. "I am worthy of giving myself time." Finding myself most mornings in the mirror face to face with myself repeating it as I got ready for my day. Awkward as hell but for some reason each day it became easier.

CHAPTER 5

Ninety percent fear

It is said that approximately ninety percent of the things we worry about, or fear *never comes true*.

That is according to Google and the various scientific studies based on fear, stated on the all-knowing internet that only ten percent of the things we fear actually happen.

As this-triggers another ah-ha moment within me to recognize that I had spent a massive portion of my life 'in my head' running through worst-case scenarios of awful outcomes that never came true. Even more jolting was that the typical scenario also included what other people's intentions were. Even as to why they did what they did as I spun a story right down to the smallest of details. Seriously, how the hell could one truly know what someone else's intentions, thoughts or reactions would be?

As I crafted these creative stories in my mind it always resulted in being let down by expectations of what people's words or reactions should or could have been. Chalking up all these elaborate stories my imagination had spun into a positive action. Almost as if to praise myself for just how creative I was. Meanwhile the real ten percent of fear I currently avoided out of my sheer disdain for discomfort.

"The only thing that needs to be fixed. Is the resistance and fear that you have created."

— Abraham Hicks.

As I start to delve into dealing with the irrational ninety percent of my fear-based daily thoughts, I begin to address fear for what it was. Just that, a thought not a fact. Not an actual event or reality, more so as just a ton of bull shit stories.

Stories that held many forms of positive and negative energy. Powerful energy that had an infinite number of options and outcomes. Outcomes that would be dictated by each and every choice that I made. Choice of thoughts, choice of words and choice of actions.

Often realising that my mind was undeniably not in line with my body or my spirit as if my thoughts literally had a mind of its own. Especially when it came to my shitty attitude and a reluctance to follow anyone else's suggestions of which was the best path to be taken.

The irrational fear began to settle in and plant seeds of doubt, in me having the ability to execute this demotion of my shitty attitude. I then try to shift and reassure myself to just keep digging. Repeating to myself that ninety percent of the things I worried about never occurred, and the other ten percent of this fear holds a true purpose. A purpose that would require one to be willing to come to terms with being uncomfortable from within while trying to embrace and find the positive side. Instead of underestimating its true power that one could achieve just by utilising fear as a tool to evolve personal growth.

It is true that fear can be unknown and irrational. Over this life span my mind had invested a serious amount of time establishing pathways based on fear. These pathways seemed to be well established and strong not unlike an old friend I would turn to in times of need.

A pathway filled with fears of not being good enough. Fears of not being loved enough. Fear of not loving others enough. Fears of what the heck am I doing? Fear over who the heck do I think I am?

Even some genuine fears over sharing this journey or the ability to create a new path of thinking seems overwhelming at times. As this path that I was on was so well travelled that I found it hard to veer onto a new one at times. Realising and analysing just how much I lived in fear shocked me.

Often leaving me with a lingering question, '*What* am I so afraid of?'

Sometimes my ego would yell, '*Nothing! It is not me. I am not afraid of anything*'. As friction appears to me, sometimes I am able to stop and breathe. Address the resistance and ask myself that important question once again, '*What* am I so afraid of?'

Strong denial and heightened negative emotions were the warning bells that I listened for as it indicated that there was definitely a supercharged emotion being held. An emotion that was dying to be released. The success of this release greatly dictates the outcome of the situation.

Driving my need to stop, take time to observe and just breathe made me hyper-aware of my thoughts.

It is not my fault, usually meant that it was me, and that part of me hated this sense of realisation. However, still I was so drawn to work through the heavy emotions the best I could. With almost a fire in my belly and a willingness to embrace these dark and yucky feelings that I had been avoiding and suppressing for so long.

Exhausted. I made my way through each release.

Quantum leaping when I started to put this into practice every moment of the day. It could be a simple snarky conversation I just had with my husband Kevin over parenting. As many parents may be able to relate to the ongoing struggle of freedom and balance. A struggle between allowing our kids to find their own way and realising that their own way may be playing video games for seven hours straight.

With my initial reaction being that I cannot believe how insensitive my husband is being and that long periods of time playing video games are damaging their very being. I realise this is simply the age-old struggle of a parent believing that their child is not doing enough. After a breath or two and asking him for a minute so that I can create space for myself to analyse what is actually going on and not what I perceive as going on.

I walk myself right out of the room I then ask myself again, 'What am I so afraid of?' Not being right. Not being accepted. Kevin not thinking I am a good parent or is it that I do not think I am a good parent?

There it is.

As I sense a heaviness cross my chest, I know I have hit a charged trapped emotion. The real reason I am so consumed with anger over my kid's bingeing on video games.

Somehow their lack of drive to do anything other than gaming is triggering in me a sense of anger and guilt. Anger of not feeling like I can control the situation and guilt of not looking like a good parent. My shitty attitude spouts on and on… 'Seriously, a good parent would never allow their child to play video games this long. They are going to grow up lazy and disrespectful with zero work ethic.'

I then remind myself that it is OK. Allow these thoughts and supercharged emotions their rightful space.

As soon as I acknowledge the charged emotions, I feel a sense of relief. Then once again I ask myself, '*What* am I so afraid of?'

'I don't want to look or feel like a bad parent. Like I did not do my job.'

Perfect! Space was now rightfully given for these emotions. As the guilt and anger start to subside, I realise this is just another example of being human. We are here to love our children and do the best we can by being the example. Their conditioning has been taught to them by us as they mimic our behaviour.

I choose to be human and reassure myself that, '*I am* a good parent and that *I am* worthy of being a good parent.' I then make my way back upstairs as Kevin's eyes and mine meet, we both smile sensing the shift. This simple shift allowed for a civil conversation between my husband and I so that we could brainstorm a plan to entice them off technology.

A conversation which in the past relied on methods of one using judgemental tones and sharp exchanges of words which had the power to consume and ruin our entire day. However, today would be different. The difference between taking a moment to breathe and finding my spark shifted our dynamics as parents.

This shift now shone a spotlight right onto the centre of this friction. Quickly and efficiently exposing it for what was, just past triggers of supercharged unexpressed emotions. Not some twisted mind-bender of a story that my thoughts wanted to take me on to fuel these trapped emotions even further. By addressing the actual situation in the present moment that our kids had been on tech for long enough was real. Instead of being angry, a simple solution would be to do something else.

A solution that involves a shift in focus regarding fear of what is happening *within me*, instead of *around me* is a game changer.

The old me would have yelled down the stairs, 'Are you going to waste the whole day playing video games?'

Only to hear crickets from their rooms followed by even more hours of gaming as they ignored me. *But* not today. The new me. This ever-evolving version of me decided to just go downstairs, ask them how their day was going and let them know that in five minutes we are all going for a swim and that we would love it if they joined us.

As I make my way through these blocked emotions happening in real-time my mind, body and spirit become more aligned. It is as if the speed and comfort with which I am dealing with present blockages that has now allowed the old blockages to come to the forefront. Understanding that it was these blockages which were exhausting me and not the present circumstance I was facing.

Reality check-in: Day 77

Mind check-in:

Trying to calm my mind and create space with some success. Reminding myself daily that my thoughts, words, and actions are powerful.

Body check-in:

Yah me. Got in one workout this week.

Spiritual check-in:

Feeling a slight connection in the quiet times.

As I integrate my daily affirmation of repeating to myself, 'My thoughts, words and actions are so powerful.'

The sheer power of thoughts, words and actions impressively impacted my ability to deal with fear. Over and over, I repeat this affirmation retraining my brain and spirit connection to be present. For if I did check out of the present moment it would relinquish power right back over to my shitty attitude. An attitude that loves to play the victim and never wants to acknowledge the gratitude set before me.

In trying to develop new mindsets and release the old ones, I sense my energy grow with each positive thought, every positive word, and every positive action as it creates newfound energy levels. A connection and power which was patiently waiting there for me to tap into it. As each connection caused a surge of energy in their own right, a ripple of energy which went out into the universe as it boomeranged right back to me.

With that feeling being held steadfast I began to question what type of ripple would I choose for myself.

Positive ripples of daily energy definitely seemed to be the optimal choice but negative mindsets and attitudes of years of conditioning would need to be addressed if I ever wanted to create a positive flow of energy on a continual basis.

A need to delve within and ask myself which energy ripple did I want to feel coming back to me?

The choice seemed obvious. Who doesn't want good things happening to them? Great conversations, joyous moments, amazing adventures, financial abundance, and present joy topped off with deep connected relationships.

As I am beginning to realise the act of wanting and doing are two very different things. As wanting leads to a sense of lack and doing leads to a sense of accomplishment. Therefore, if this is all true, no wonder most of my days seem to entail some sort of chaos.

"What goes around, comes around." — Unknown

This old adage of what goes around comes around sparked a newfound understanding. This simple yet profound statement creates a connection and understanding of the true power and weight of influence for the energy that we generate and receive.

Being a visual learner with a love of the outdoors, I began to create a picture in my mind of two buckets. One for negative and one for positive. Each thought, word and action represented by a pebble found which would then be placed into its rightful bucket throughout my day. Much like a child collecting treasures at the beach. Some small, some big, some shiny, some covered in muck.

Taking note at the end of my day of the sheer level that each bucket had been filled. This intention is to observe the placement over the need for all thoughts to be positive allowing me without judgement to understand simply where I was placing my energy.

On a wonderful day, it felt as if that positive bucket overflowed with shiny beach glass and smooth pebbles. However, more importantly, I acknowledged on a rough day a sense of needing a larger negative bucket as the jagged muck encrusted rocks spilt over the rim.

This realisation as to where I was placing this energy now generated a clear sense as to why the gripping sadness had such a hold on me. As my negative bucket tended to be filled at a much quicker rate only to be taken to the shore chucking the bucket and all into the water. Fired up watching as the pebbles ejected out onto the surface of the water causing the water to spray up and sting my eyes as the chaos of an even larger splash from the bucket itself drenched me.

With this realisation that often after a negative experience I was not taking any claim to the fact that it was me who threw the bucket in the first place. Or more so how these negative actions often caused a negative chain reaction.

However, once in a blue moon, I had a full positive bucket that I then meticulously poured out onto the shoreline reminiscing back on each experience throughout my day. These actions started to create something new as each pebble caused the surface of the water to create a beautiful infinite ripple. It radiated in all directions kissing my fingertips as the water's ripple danced its way back to me.

Sometimes it was easy to make a positive choice and sometimes it was a blatant choice to make a negative splash. The real question would be which of these choices would I want to come back to me now that I understood and accepted the simple principle of the law of attraction as a real-life application.

Recognizing the importance to just observe and not judge my current state of being as a bad place or bad thoughts, but as a work in progress with the goal of upgrading a current state. Ultimately observing without judgement would result in the ability to super-size my positive bucket as well.

Implementing choice in a sort of messy configuration as I baby-stepped my way through all of these questions, I acknowledge that the majority of days are filled with both positive and negative energy which have the ability to either make or break my day.

So how did a hard day make me feel? Well, it currently felt as if nothing was going right, utterly exhausting, extremely frustrated as my mind filled with judgement and hurt feelings leaving me face down in the foetal position in the sand. Fighting off the feeling to flee and deal with this situation another day.

Even as I document this journey, I admit that if I go down that path of putting it off for 'another day' that 'day' never comes because negativity loves itself much like positive energy loves itself. Like attracting like.

This was abundantly clear that a hard day was an actual struggle which brought me to assess how good days feel. Effortless, easy, energised and filled with great situations that seemed to just happen right before my eyes.

Explain this to me then, how exactly is being positive and having a good day hard?

How is thinking, speaking, and acting positive so hard? Obviously, this was some seriously flawed theory which has been conditioned into my mind. The simple fact was that when things were going right everything seemed almost effortlessly. This shone the light on how brainwashed I was to view situations negatively.

It was this simple concept that I had the opportunity to make a choice each time no matter the situation.

Observing my mindset opened my eyes up to see just how rooted my negative state of mind was as I utilised this simple tool of reflection. A visualisation exercise of going to the beach would allow for a hard reset of my mindset to take root.

'*The beach*'.

Let's say you loved the beach (just go with it). You plan a big day trip to your favourite lake that you go to each year and have been looking forward to all week. You wake up feeling energised and excited for your big day at the beach. You are feeling completely prepared as you pack up all your favourite foods, snacks, beach toys, sunshade, towels, etc. Everyone then piles into the car. You stop to fill up with gas as you set out on your road trip.

Everyone is excited as you spend the whole drive enjoying some great music and conversation. Arriving early, you find the perfect parking spot then proceed to unload everyone out of the car feeling the blissful heat of the sun warming your back.

Then you all make your way across the beautiful sandy beach and feel the warmth of the sun kiss your face as you breathe in the sweet fresh air coming off the water. You arrive at your favourite spot, fluffing out your extra-large beach blanket. As you claim your beloved spot on the beach which is idyllically half in the sun and half in the shade of a beautiful oak tree. You then spend the day with friends and family laughing, eating, napping, swimming, and soaking up the warm sun. It is glorious.

About an hour before you are ready to pack up for the day the wind picks up and dark clouds start to roll in. In a feverous whirlwind of sand-pelting wind, you all frantically pack up your belongings. Your beach day has abruptly come to an end. As the sky opens up and the rain starts to pour, everyone with arms full races back to the car utterly soaked.

Now check in with your mind. How was your trip to the beach? How did it start? How did it end? Did you mind veer off?

We will all have a different experience with this sort of visualisation exercise. I know I did, I paused only to blurt out, "Oh crap."

Recalling that with-in the first sentence I had already dreamed up the nightmare of getting everyone and everything organised as we packed up the car. Then followed by some brief fighting and the silent treatment that ensued as we made our way to a packed beach. Only then to find that the beach blanket I brought was too small and that I should have brought a bigger one. However, we did have fun and ate too many treats and got too much sun. Ultimately ending up back in the car upset that it rained ruining the day.

This was a clear indication that my mind's *set-point* was most definitely set on negative. Not only was my set-point at negative, but it was creating fear out of nothing. A simple visualisation story had the ability to induce stress and charged emotions. For someone who prided themselves on being positive and always trying to see the bright side of things, this shone a light on reality as I had the ability to turn even a positive experience into a negative one.

As I take a deep breath in, I remind myself that we are all human repeating in my head, *Do not judge, just observe and make a better choice next time.*

I decided to try this visualisation exercise again this time with the full intention of simply listening to the words as they start to create a picture in my mind, allowing only the emotions associated with those words to flow. Releasing a little more of my shitty attitude's ability to turn light into darkness as I refuse to allow my mind to derail me this time. Noting at the end of the exercise that my mind did trail off. However, this time the story developed into an enjoyable exercise that I would have loved to spend the day at the beach. Right down to seeing everyone run through the rain bursting into laughter as we loaded ourselves into the car at the sight of each other's rain-drenched hair.

I sit here now feeling grateful for this amazing gift that this exercise has brought me. Once again confirming that I was one step closer to releasing this sadness. Sure, the first time I did this visualisation exercise my mind went crazy but being honest with myself is what created this shift as I accepted every last negative imagery I had created. Bringing my attention that once again I had been spending my life always focused on what went wrong. Instead of that went right, verifying that my conditioning was deeply rooted in fear.

A fear which ultimately resulted in making others and myself feel less than the best version of ourselves. As my mission became clear that in order to address fear, I could focus on bringing out the best in myself and others when faced with uncomfortable or negative situations.

Bringing it back to the present moment as I ask myself, 'What is actually happening in this very moment?' Replacing my warped interpretation of what I think is happening becomes an invaluable tool as I document my journey of reconnecting with my spark. A spark that would be greatly challenged as this year would globally bring fear to the forefront.

"Sometimes our lives have to be completely shaken up. Changed. And rearranged to relocate us to the place we're meant to be." — Unknown.

Thursday, March eleven, 2020: Day eighty-one.

It happened.

In my mind, March eleven, 2020, was the day the pandemic hit Canada, also known as the life-changing dreaded *COVID-19*. The day Covid-19 became exceedingly real after a few weeks prior to hearing the reports from China, Italy, and other parts of the world about some mysterious virus.

Honestly, it seemed to be tragic, but this distant virus did not seem to be a very big deal. A flu which thankfully

Canada had only a few rare cases of which was not impacting me or my family. I somehow felt as if I was detached much like a bystander watching some sci-fi movie from the comfort of my couch. However, on March eleven our provincial government announced that schools would be closed for two extra weeks after the March break. *OK, no big deal* I thought. I guess I will be working from home and the kids will just set up a little home-school schedule. What is all the fuss about? Little did I realise what was to come.

Later that week, after attempting to finalise plans for my in-law's celebratory 50th wedding anniversary dinner, we cancelled. After numerous phone calls within the family, a group decision was made to cancel our reservation due to this weird new suggestion that people social distance. Not even sure at the time what this foreign concept of social distancing was and why everyone was overreacting.

No problem. Jen to the rescue. The solution is simple: we can just host the family here! After all, fiftieth wedding anniversaries do not come along every day. I then proceeded to run out to the store to grab a cake mix and a few other items for the celebration. As I arrived at our local grocery store, I sensed an overwhelming amount of fear and panic in the air.

Customers were lined up thirty people deep, heads down, eyes fixed on their phones with shopping carts overflowing. Weird, I knew that there was a lot of talk of this new flu bug and that our kids were staying home a little longer than expected but what the hell was going on?

Feeling like maybe I had missed something or that the government was totally overreacting by enforcing these new safety measures made me even more determined not to join in this frenzy. Aimlessly I began to wander around the store speculating as to why all these crazy people-were overloading their carts with canned goods and toilet paper.

Seriously people every year the flu kills thousands of people, and this year's virus in particular-seemed to be a nasty one. As I push my own cart around, the heavy energy in the store begins to take hold of me. Sensing the grip of this intense energy I take a deep breath in trying to create a bubble around myself only to feel it pop as I exhale. Sending me into a shopping frenzy as if my life depended on it all the while trying not to have any eye contact with people as I overloaded my own cart. The next thing I knew, I was that crazy person who came for a cake mix and left with ten bags of groceries and a hefty bill.

Feeling embarrassed I then quickly loaded my groceries into the back of my car, hoping that no one I knew saw my panicked frenzy. I then got into the driver's seat and just sat there, stunned. *What the hell just happened?*

Feelings of overwhelming panic and stress washed in again gripping tighter and tighter as I reflected back to what exactly just transpired. Tapping into all the emotions and thoughts I had just experienced. That is when it happened fear went wild with excitement like my shitty attitude was just gifted the best Christmas present ever as I flashed back to my experience in the store.

What if the grocery store closes? What if I could not feed my own children? What if we starved to death? What if this is the start of the end of the world? What if I died? What if my children died?

As my thoughts began to derail, they were topped off with feelings of guilt and shame that I too was panicking as I overfilled my shopping cart. I begin to feel the build-up of pressure making-its way across my chest and tears now glide down my face knowing that the best thing I could do was allow these large emotions their rightful place. However, I sensed a dire need to stop. Stop feeling sorry for myself. Get it together I tell myself, as I start the car and make my way home.

I realised I could not enter my home in this state, so I stuffed it all down and put on my happy face as I entered the house. I found myself laughing and commenting that I may have gone a little crazy with the groceries today saying nothing to relieve the pressure inside of me.

As the days slowly dragged out and conspiracies of governments pitting against each other, and that this virus was man-made by joint ventures of power-hungry leaders who were looking to create one currency and one immunisation to take over the world continue to trickle out. It was hard to know what to believe or what to feel. Being present and true to what was happening around me became virtually impossible. As I will be the first to admit, my mind was definitely spiralling down that Covid rabbit hole into a pit of despair.

After days of feeling dreadful, I remind myself just how good it felt only a few weeks earlier to be connected especially when shit got bad. Admitting to myself that I have come so far as I literally have just dug myself out of my own pity-party rabbit hole so there was no way in hell I was going to let even a pandemic take this newfound freedom away from me.

After all, this was my year of awakening. An awakening to healing. After all, friction is just something that is drawing my attention to something that needs to be addressed. Not ignored. As my present state was a glaring reminder of just what happens when one ignores their emotions.

I had a choice, a really, really, really big one.

A choice to live in fear and follow the social media bombardment with Covid-19 or I could turn inward and focus on what really meant everything to me. Peace, love, and positive impact. However, in order to do that I am required to repeat some of the steps that have taken me this far.

After all, if it worked prior with proven results then why could it not work now with this same sort of shit just a different pile.

Going back to the basics of using my breath as I observed and feel without judgement brings it all back to this very moment. As I sat on my couch looking out over the water, I asked myself one simple question, '*What* is happening at this very moment?'

Nothing, really nothing was actually happening. I was healthy and safe, and my family was healthy and safe. I felt a small spark of warmth in my chest, but it quickly fizzled as I started to address how this whole COVID-19 business is making me feel.

Frankly, I was scared shitless for my kid's safety. In addition to my husband and our extended family's safety as well as my own made way for fear to creep in with vivid images of us staring in the walking dead.

Obviously, I am scared shitless of the unknown and accept that I consciously need to allow these feelings to flow. They need to have their rightful place in order for me not to trap all these big emotions within my body. I take in a deep breath and let my eyes gaze back out to the water. I feel my chest tighten and a lump makes its way up my throat as tears stream down my face. I burst into an ugly cry, sobbing uncontrollably as the tension is released with each wave of emotion.

About twenty minutes after I opened these floodgates my mind and body were exhausted from expressing these heavy emotions with nothing left to give. I laid back on the couch only thinking about my breath as my mind began to settle and become quiet. Following my breath as it entered peacefully into my lungs and flowed right down to the tips of my toes dissolving any lingering stress as I exhaled. In and out repeating this healing breath.

Reality check-in.

Mind check-in:

Covid-19. Mind blown. Panic. Cry. Pick myself back up, rinse and repeat.

Body check-in:

Random stomach pains remind me of my childhood issue of what stress can do if trapped in a little body. Negative energy = negative suppressed emotion = pain in my belly. Reminder to allow, feel and breath.

Spiritual check-in:

Shaken. Seriously shaken but feeling slightly relieved having made a choice with Covid.

Tonight's journaling session was cut short as my phone rang.

It was my sister crying; her brother-in-law had died from Covid-19. *What!* I thought only the sick and old people had a slim chance of dying from this flu bug as I demanded more details. My mind screamed as she spoke as if my hair was lit on fire with the burning questions that raged through my mind to find reason within all this chaos.

Was he travelling or sick before all of this? No, he was at a medical conference. Was he old? No, he was in his early sixties.

Shit just got real as I tried to console my sister, I could not stop thinking about her and how this would devastate their entire family. To make matters worse, she now informs me that days prior to his death his sons in their twenties had come to check in on their sick dad. They too tested positive for Covid-19 and were now struggling to recover. What, but they are in their twenties.

I hung up the phone after a short conversation and I felt the tears well up, my chest tightens, and my stomach began to twist into a knot. I must not crumble; I must be strong. Is this real, am I dreaming? I could barely look my husband in the eyes as I knew I would instantly fall apart. We quickly tucked our kids into bed, giving them some extra hugs and kisses, telling them that everything was fine as I rushed out of their bedrooms into my husband's arms to have a good cry.

The sheer panic of the unknown hit me like a ton of bricks causing me to sob uncontrollably as he squeezed me tight in his arms. After allowing these emotions their rightful place I looked up into my husband's eyes for reassurance. Reassurance, which was always there, but instead all I saw was sadness and fear as well.

For some reason, this did not freak me out. It instantly shocked me right out of my own emotional pity party and into a clear head space with a jolt. Slapping my face sharply with his empty sad eyes. This jolt allowed me to acknowledge that I was indeed going down that rabbit hole of despair.

STOP Jen, just stop, and breathe, I reassured myself over and over.

Clarity started to resurface with each conscious breath reminding me that all I required was to bring my mind back to this present moment. Right here, right now. I had but only one job to do.

Be present.

I began asking myself, "What is happening right now at this very moment?" Currently, at this very moment, I am healthy, my kids are healthy, and my husband is healthy. We both have steady jobs. A roof over our heads, and money to pay bills. With these simple thoughts of gratitude, it slowly started to replace and override the grief, stress, and sadness with space and clarity.

"Have patience with all things but chiefly have patience with yourself. Do not lose courage in considering your own imperfections but instantly set about remedying them - every day begin the task anew."

— Saint Francis de Sales.

The very words every day, begin the task anew has fostered a profound shift for me.

At the end of each day, I started to feel a sense of awakening or enlightenment. Yet, each day as I awoke it was as if I had forgotten where I left off as if the process was in itself starting anew.

This year of healing myself would be the beginning of truly evolving my personal growth and connection through all raw and rough situations. Some days my emotional rollercoaster took over with a vengeance lasting what seemed like infinity. Taking me for a wide emotional ride for the entire day while others would last just a few moments.

The pandemic had brought about an unpredictable stress. Stress regarding our future. I was not used to stressing about the future as for so many years I had lived in the past. Yet, now, it threw me into the future whether I wanted to be there or not. Bringing forth many questions I had never taken the time to worry about.

"What if we both got sick? What if I died? What if we both died? Who would look after our kids? How would that impact our kids? What if we both lost our jobs? Lost our house? Then we would not be able to buy groceries to feed our children."

Usually, at this point of my downward spiral, I started to feel nauseous and the pain in my belly ripped through me as it merged with some heavy chest pain. Understanding now that this pain was a signal to be present. Trying to remind myself that this was the universe giving me a serious warning sign in my body to chill the fuck out and just breathe.

The friction of this newfound stress was real, like all horrible situations I had a choice to suffer or dig deep to find strength and perseverance to make my way out of it. Or at least find a new way to search for peace amongst the chaos.

With everything turning upside down we had to adjust to all the new ways of life. Socialising. Not socialising. School. No schooling. Online school. Shopping. Limited shopping. Jobs going online to people losing their jobs.

The chaos forced me to find a new way to dig deep and find the positive in this shitty situation. Frankly, it was a new unbelievable world situation.

With a realisation that just because Covid was taking over the world it did not need to take over our home. After all, I only have control over where I am at and how I feel at this very moment. Therefore, if I wanted happiness to still be a big part of each day I needed to just keep trying. Determined but having little to no idea how this wonderful plan could happen especially since fear was gaslighting my rational thoughts at every turn.

CHAPTER 6

Make the damn choice

The beauty of choice is that when deciding what to do next in a difficult situation we are presented with an infinite number of possibilities whether we acknowledge that fact or not.

Like many growing up, I felt as if I never had a choice. Convincing myself that I was condemned to a life of being forced along for the ride. A ride reminiscent of being in a hot car as a passenger sitting in the back seat without a seatbelt being tossed around with each turn. I did have high hopes that someone would notice that I was overheating, battered and in need of stopping for a breath of fresh air and food, or at least roll down the window for me.

Only they never did, no window unrolled, never stopping as they abandoned me in the back seat to suffer in silence feeling sorry for myself. Never did I utter a word to express that I was on the brink of heat stroke or that I did not like my present situation resulting in overwhelming feelings of loneliness. Never choosing to speak up declaring my need to stop, never realising I always had that god given choice to choose.

As I fast forward to today, I realise these deep-rooted feelings of helplessness were still an integral part of my belief system. As I found myself starting each day with a positive mindset never seemed to be enough as the next thing I knew, someone would come along and ruin it. This brought about an essential need to address this mindset of giving others the ability to ruin and influence my own behaviour was eminent.

It is true that one does not always have control over outcomes but damn it, if they say I have an infinite number of choices on how I would react then I am determined to at least explore what these so-called other choices may bring.

Since 'they' in all their wisdom say that happiness is a choice but living it daily can be another thing, especially in a pandemic. A pandemic that had the ability to make life seem overwhelming, frantic, and fleeting as it continually brought up fears of death, life, and my own self-worth in this world. Shining a spotlight on what I had accomplished but especially what I had not accomplished with my life thus far.

In doing nothing during this pandemic I was choosing pity, fear, and self-doubt. An observation that came with clarity as life began to shift and overreactions began to settle. A shifting into problem-solving day in and day out as I made a point to observe my shitty attitude's addition to being a problem-maker.

It seems obvious that no one would willingly choose unhappiness. Yet, that is exactly what I had been doing numerous times a day as I constantly fostered what made me unhappy. Instead of focusing and reminiscing on what brought me happiness. I seemed to be nit-picking my way through life over all the small details as I allowed myself to be consumed.

As I navigate through my newfound choices news of death tolls and devastation settled into our home. It is like a thick fog making its way through the smallest of cracks as it began to invade our space. Weeks into social distancing and self-isolation as death tolls now rising to sixty thousand worldwide exceeding the average annual number of people who have died from the flu each year.

An abrupt comprehension that this was no longer your typical flu bug as Canada's death toll rose to over three hundred which compared to other countries was excellent but was giving me little to no comfort. I remind myself that I cannot change what is happening in the world however I do have the ability in my own life to shift with small changes. Knowing that each small change to my mindset would add up to a better mood and better choices, especially when faced with chaos.

Each day I attempted to change up some of my daily tasks, the way I brushed my teeth, the amount of news I consumed, and even when I went for groceries. A single shift of deciding to change my weekly grocery run from a Saturday to a weeknight in hopes of avoiding the negative energy of frantic consumers made a noticeable difference.

I know this sounds like a ridiculously small thing, but like most people, I have completed life's tasks like grocery shopping the same day and around the same time for years, as if on cruise control.

No real thought or purpose for this meaningful act of having the privilege of grocery shopping with a somewhat unlimited budget or the flexibility of time to go whichever evening I desired.

These small changes started to feel so good even the way I looked at the most mundane tasks, such as getting groceries seemed to fuel my spark from within. As not so long ago being consumed with the anxiety of having to go masked up and deal with the energy in the grocery store seemed overwhelming.

I kept reminding myself that it is a privilege to be grateful to be able to afford to buy groceries as many people were now losing their jobs, businesses, and livelihoods. The economical strain now seemed bigger than any virus, but these news reports were only distractions to pull me off track.

"Each of us will emerge, in our own way, from this storm.

It is very important to see beyond what is seen at first glance. Not just looking, actually seeing."

— Unknown

As the covid storm brewed and the sense of urgency of needing to fix the cracks which were allowing the pandemic to stream into our home turned into small acts of what change can I do today.

Raising that question of what truly made me feel happy.

It always seemed to come down to the simple things in life like watching my kids play, hearing them laugh, taking a hot shower, having a positive conversation or sharing a homecooked meal. These were all things that I recognized as having the ability to calm my mind and create a spark within as it loosened the grip of sadness momentarily.

Knowing today of all days I would need to dig deep and make a positive choice as I made my way to the hospital to visit my dear friend, Linda, who was once again admitted for complications due to her stage four terminal lung cancer.

As I stood outside her room garbing myself with a hospital gown, face mask and gloves I take in a deep breath and remind myself to be strong as I enter her room. Her husband Lanny is off in the corner reading something on his phone and Linda is hyper-focused on her television screen as she does not notice me as I walk in.

"Hello", I blurt out nervously way too loud as I am sure the whole floor thought I was addressing them. Linda flinches, swinging her head in my direction as our eyes meet, detecting her energy shift as her eyes light up. At that moment, I felt sheer gratitude for being able to visit her as there has been talk of restricting visitors at the hospital due to the pandemic.

I centre myself and take in a deep cleansing breath. Fully aware that the local news is running on a loop as her eyes shift from me back to the television as the broadcaster belts out new death tolls leaving its echo in my ears. I try to concentrate on our conversation finding myself struggling with being present.

Choices, I remind myself. Attempting to shift the conversation to anything but Covid, I decide to pull out my phone and share a few pictures of my kids playing in the snow a few months prior.

As the conversation then falls silent, her husband Lanny pipes up that he is going downstairs to get a cup of coffee and I once again see Linda's eyes light up. I too get excited with her shift of energy and curious about what seems so pressing to discuss with me now that Lanny is leaving the room.

As quickly as her eyes had lit up, her energy and state became very serious as she began to express all her concerns about how Lanny will fare once she is gone. As I held her hand, she began to voice her concerns one by one about him being alone. The questions ensued of: Who will take care of him? And how would he fare without her? I began to reassure her that we have and always will be here for both of them and that that would never change even if life did.

The room went silent as it began to fill with the energy of unconditional love and devotion between two friends and for the first time, I noticed the yellowish-grey hue of her face become glaringly apparent.

An hour later we wrap up our visit and I made my way back to the car. With each step fighting off the tears only to breakdown once I reached my car door. Plunking myself down in the driver's seat as I allow my emotions to erupt as feelings of sheer sorrow for Lanny living alone and the very real possibility of Linda no longer being part of my life, floods over me.

In the past I would have only allowed myself a tear or two before stuffing down all the emotions and moving on to thoughts of mundane tasks, never embracing or allowing sadness its rightful space. Permitting this flood of emotions to overtake me as I secured myself in the present moment of allowing. Once I clearly sensed the poignant heaviness across my chest being relieved by being present and providing adequate space to feel all the emotions, I decide it is now time to head home.

I start the car and before I can put it into drive my phone rings and it is my husband Kevin checking to see how my visit went as if he sensed my pain and sorrow. Kevin then explained he felt a need to call but was in no way trying to rush me causing me to weep once again but this time because I acknowledged we were connecting on a deeper level.

Through my newly erupted sobs, I begin to share Linda's heartfelt conversation which had resulted in my present state as he listened and expressed his support. As we wrapped up our discussion, I once again began to feel the rush of gratitude for his support and awareness of Linda's meaningful conversation.

Making my way home as the lines on the highway flicker, lulling me into a state of, 'what can I do to help in this shitty situation'. Feelings of helplessness would be so easy to feed into but I am determined to embrace choice within all of this chaos of cancer which abruptly points out that life is short, and each day is truly a gift.

Admitting to myself there is simply no way for me to heal or fix Linda so what else could I do? It was time to get creative as thoughts of gratitude for my own health and my family's health washed over me. These thoughts of gratitude for one's health were good, but I knew it was also self-centred with the potential to trigger self-pity. With this awareness of where my mind was wanting to travel, I began to think outside of myself.

If I could not fix this situation, then what could I do or give? My shitty attitude pipped in that 'seriously you have nothing to give and there is no way shape or form that you can fix any part of this terrible situation'. As I observe these thoughts, I take in a deep breath to create space and realise that I do have a choice and something to give. As helping another person comes in so many forms of giving without the need to fix but to support them relieving the pressure of the situation momentarily has the ability to create a positive space.

As the days passed everything started to shift, I felt an even stronger pull to embrace giving possibly because it is a simple act that anyone can do. A simple act of giving which is universal and can be done by anyone, for anyone, of any age, anywhere. Giving can be as simple or complex. This act of giving may be through your time, your patience, your attention, your abundance or even your kind words. Especially powerful the act of giving when there is no expectation of thanks or recognition is one of my favourite unconditional gestures of love.

I almost felt somewhat guilty over just how good it made me feel and how quickly it relinquished the need to control and fix the situation. Simply just the act of exchanging positive energy and feeling the power of that flow as I began to tap its true power. I have come to think that the art of giving is also a sort of therapy that a person can offer up to themselves. On days that I seem to be consumed with negative thoughts of anxiety and feeling of sadness, I turn my attention to random acts of kindness.

"If you knew what I know about the power of giving, you would not let a single meal pass without sharing it in some way" — Unknown.

Through all this digging into the root cause of my shitty attitude, I have discovered that one of my favourite ways of giving is through cooking. This simple process of the creation of a meal itself is what seems to make the gesture of giving more meaningful for me. It simply amazes me the power of a jar of homemade jam, soup or a hot meal had especially during a pandemic.

After all, soup is good for the soul, so they say. Who does not enjoy eating a warm bowl of comfort? I love the simple act of making something from scratch with fresh ingredients and sealing it up in recycled glass jars to give away. At first, my husband Kevin would ask me, 'Why are you giving our food away?' Do not judge him, you have to understand the man loved his leftovers. My reply was always the same: because I can. In doing something good it also makes me feel good which in return makes a positive ripple right back to my own family. Plus, what better way to get out of a funk and into a positive mindset?

Soup for me represented so much more than just food as growing up my mom would have a pot of soup simmering on the stovetop weekly. Even in a home that did not show love openly, I knew that making soup was definitely good for her soul as I reflect back on the positive way it provided comfort to my family.

I think because this was such a common occurrence at the time, I took it for granted. However, now as an adult learning to cook for myself soup was an easy comfort meal which could be enjoyed by all.

To this day my mom and I love to share new soup recipes, it has become such a pivotal way of giving and receiving love between two people. Cooking not only is an essential skill but in my mind is one of the greatest gifts you can share with your loved ones. Having everyone gather around for a good meal and conversation is priceless, which I know it sounds so cliché, but it is so true. Many fond memories of mine have been made hanging around the kitchen table eating a meal with loved ones and enjoying each other's company.

Therefore, my goal in spite of all the chaos happening around me is to try to find as many simple acts of kindness as possible. Giving began to create its own mission bringing me something so pure, positive, and totally unexpected, it brought me joy. The more I became present in giving the more I enjoyed the process of what I was giving whether it be making soup, jars of jam, or doing a porch drop-off.

This would be one of the most positive life lessons Covid has taught me. A valuable lesson that choice matters and can make a difference.

As with each jar delivered, I also felt a warm hug of energy that resonated between us from within. Especially today's drop-off for Linda who was now home but not able to take any visitors and is resting. This delivery ended with a swift social distance visit with her husband Lanny outside as he embraces the love that could mutually be felt.

A smile, a kind word, small gestures and even making soup all started to add up to me having more positive days than negative.

Reality check-in: Day 111

Mind check-in:

Power struggle over my mind and my spirit is real and only shows how separate they currently are.

Body check-in:

Doing more meditation and walks than exercise but I will take it.

Spiritual check-in:

Feeling more content in quiet moments however acknowledging fear has amplified the sadness.

For the last few days, I have been trying to keep the sadness at bay. I head upstairs to enjoy the last few hours of my long weekend.

Our phone began to ring, it was Lanny calling to say that my dear friend Linda had died last night at home in her sleep after her long battle with cancer. An instant feeling of relief for her suffering finally ending washed over me followed by a flood of emotions as I listened to him speak.

Our all too brief conversation quickly came to an end as we were both falling apart on the phone. 'Oh my God', is all I could think for this poor man, not only did his wife just die but his dog a few weeks earlier. This beautiful couple were childless and the weight of his impending loneliness and loss was so heavy in his voice that it still rang in my ears as I hung up the phone.

My heart felt like it was literally breaking. Breaking into pieces over not having the ability to just rush over to their house and hug him, but no. I cannot as this fucking Covid situation was becoming more than I could handle some days with social distancing rules being strictly enforced.

I feel anger starting to rage within as I share the news of Linda's passing with Kevin. Vocalizing my frustration of not being able to better support Lanny especially after having reassured Linda that we would be there for him. Topping off my rage with the ridiculous inability to even have a funeral. Allowing myself to acknowledge the rage but not fuel it. I remind myself that this event is not about me and that situations can always be made worse by the path that I was about to choose.

Asking myself to make a choice to take a path of giving or a path of taking and for some reason this always seems to shock me out of my own pity party. My fear and rage become tears of gratitude for her having touched our lives.

Moments later my kids make their way up for breakfast, they stop dead in their tracks as they realise that I have been crying as Kevin breaks the news to them of their dear friend Linda's death. Speechless with tears streaming down my cheeks a shift in energy felt by us all sent us into a seriously long silent family hug. A hug only to be broken by my daughter's comment that she has only seen me cry once in her life. Shocking me once more into the reality of how much I had suppressed my hidden emotions. Even the most human of emotions were hidden from my own family as I made sure to keep the surface of my life looking perfect and calm at all times.

We then reminisced over all the great memories we had spent with Linda and Lanny lounging around their pool, swimming, and laughing away the afternoon. This was followed by more tears shed, however, this time they were tears of gratitude that our paths had crossed and that we were blessed with so many great memories. I mention that after breakfast I would love to go down to the lake and say a few words for Linda seeing as there would be no funeral that we could attend. My young daughter, Makayla suggested that we write on rocks all the things we loved about Linda and then we could throw them into the water. As she spoke and I felt her energy radiate pure love. A love that flooded over me once again with a mix of relief and strangely joy.

I do love when my kid's creative acts of kindness naturally show through as this was obviously a useful tool that impacted my daughter. A tool which we introduced to her a few years prior in order to move through her own painful period in life. We had her write all her hurt feelings and emotions that a bully was causing her. As to this day, she remembers writing on the rock and then carrying it around with her for a week or two to make sure all those hurt feelings were expressed.

Then the day came when she told us she was ready to let it go, so we motored to the middle of the lake where she dropped the rock into the deep dark waters. I still remember to this day her comment that she should have picked a bigger rock reminding me even today that releasing pain can take time. I thanked her for the inspiring idea, as we all headed down to the water with markers and rocks in hand.

We then began decorating the rock as we shared all the cherished memories Linda had gifted us. We took a few pictures of all the dedication rocks we created for Linda, so that we could print out and give the picture to Lanny. Knowing that a funeral would not be possible during this time of Covid we wanted to ensure him that the impact of Linda's life would not be forgotten.

Then we proceeded to throw all the dedication rocks far into the water accompanied by a few more tears. The sorrow of her dying started to turn to eternal gratefulness as I was profoundly grateful that she was no longer suffering and that her new adventure was just beginning.

Wondering if one day she would come back to visit me in a new form. So, as the year passed, I would notice out my window a fluffy robin sitting on the patio railing watching me work. Every time this happens, I always say hi to Linda and thank her for the visit.

Linda's passing as I am sure with all deaths made me extremely appreciative of my own life and just how short and fleeting it can be. My only goal and purpose in this life is to feel that I lived it to the fullest, loved to the fullest, laughed to the fullest and that I gave to the fullest.

With the death of Linda also came a mix of so many feelings. Feelings of sadness, anxiety, fear, gratitude, and hope as I work through all these emotions. I realise that happiness is not an emotion it is more of a state of mind or place in time. When someone dies the impact is a measurement of how it affects our individual happiness, missing them, wanting them, even feeling bad for others whose happiness is also affected by this loss.

"The only true loss is the loss of happiness." — Unknown.

Gratitude, thankfulness, or love is defined as a feeling of appreciation felt by the recipient whether it be a gift, gesture, or kind words. As I establish the habit of starting my day with a few thoughts of gratitude it appears to be flawed.

It was as if my thoughts of gratitude started off as your run-of-the-mill thanks. I am grateful for my home, my family, my health, my job, blah, blah but I knew if I truly wanted a lasting shift from within it required juicy details to charge up positive energy and healing. Not a superficial run of mill zombie like gratitude.

This was when the magic started to happen. If my focus of gratitude was health than the more, I acknowledged each juicy detail of what exactly I was grateful for, the fewer aches and pains I experienced. As awkward as it was, I made my way from head to toe focusing on gratitude. As many little details of my body that I was grateful for such as my strong legs being able to carry me, or my heart that was capable of carrying me through a CrossFit workout, right down to my intuitive sense of touch.

Opening the door to an understanding that the real gift that I was given was the gift of life and that waking up each day was not certain. Acknowledging that to date I only expected a daily guarantee to wake up and experience another day often without any real intention or purpose other than pleasing myself by completing tasks. The unappreciated precious gift which in the past I had taken for granted as many mornings began grudgingly getting up to start my day as if it was my God-given right that I would be alive.

This pivotal realization that these begrudging days had left me in a deep depression of lack, a lack of love, motivation, and abundance but now I had a choice to start my day differently. An ah-ha moment which also inundated my thoughts of past conditioning of continually not being good enough was abruptly squashed by reminding myself to observe without judgement.

I took a deep breath.

I began creating a much-needed space to forgive myself as we are continually evolving. Sensing the sheer gratitude for being given another day to evolve and grow through the inspiration of the present moment no matter how small or insignificant I thought it was at the time. It is these little things that had the ability to add up, creating a massive positive ripple in my life.

Noting the vast importance of getting up and going to bed each night with thoughts of gratitude as I dig my way through each layer of sadness.

CHAPTER 7

To forgive or not to forgive, that is the question

Forgiveness is defined as an intentional and voluntary process where one may initially feel victimized or undergoes a change in feelings and attitude regarding a given offence in which they are now able to overcome negative emotions such as resentment and vengeance however justified these emotions might have been.

Yes, this is a mouth full as even the definition of forgiveness streams a vast array of emotions, questions, and memories deep seeded in the need to complete this important action.

Raising questions such as: how does one go about truly forgiving? When does one deserve to be forgiven?

All I can say is that forgiveness was and still is a process.

A process which often needs to evolve over time unfolding in small, long-drawn-out increments. While other times forgiveness is similar to ripping off a band-aid, painful, and quick with a rush of relief and peace once it was done. As I explore my feelings around forgiveness, I quickly realised that it is easy to see how forgiveness can be an essential part of growth. However, growth and willingness do not always go hand and hand.

I needed to stop and observe without judgement, reminding myself just how far I had already come regarding forgiveness. My ego frequently stepped in insisting that I did not hold a grudge and that I was at ease with moving forward from all situations but my spirit with its soft guiding voice would remind me to observe forgiveness in its true form without judgement. Prompting me to dig into all my conditioning around the feelings that come up pertaining to forgiveness.

As I navigated my way to forgive those in my life, I realised growing up that I had no idea what forgiveness was and how to do it.

My conditioned belief system that had formed around forgiveness was seriously flawed mainly because it centred around withholding forgiveness than the actual act of forgiving. Labelling me a 'non-forgiver'. *'Non-forgiver'* is a person who is unwilling to make the choice to forgive. Who makes the choice not to overcome feelings of resentment but would rather carry the pain than release it.

If you are currently questioning the validity of this word and definition you would be correct as I have invented this creative word 'non-forgiver' to suit and describe my state of forgiveness.

It best describes the conditioned state in which I had spent the earlier part of my life, a time when forgiveness was required to be earned and was greatly dependent on the other person's actions. The other person who would be sequestered to do some sort of perfect act of contrition in order for them to gain my precious forgiveness. This made for a seemingly impossible feat.

Most belief systems and processes when dealing with hurt are based on flawed and impossible actions. Each generation passing on these belief systems to their young as a way of life.

The 'non-forgiver' had similar survival traits and tactics as it continued down each generation looking to protect itself as it accumulated power and strength. After all, it is the survival of the fittest, or so we are conditioned to think with an incessant drive to make our way through life at any cost.

However, what if the survival of the fittest true purpose meant digging deeper into the uncomfortable situations of life instead of fighting them?

As I delved into the conditioning that I was holding over forgiveness I realised that the passing on of the 'non-forgiver' trait was strong in our family lineage. A survival trait which would prove its longevity and strength in my father's generation.

The 'non-forgiver' trait had very distinct characteristics. It coveted forgiveness in the same way as a rare jewel, passing it on from parent to child. Each generation vividly giving examples of how to covet this rare jewel demanding it to be protected at all costs. As the 'non-forgiver' obsessed over this rare jewel of forgiveness never letting it out of site. Holding it tight in the same way as Gollum from Lord of the Rings with only one law to rule it.

O

Forgiveness was to be admired but never spent as we kept it safe almost like life itself depended on it.

As a child, my dad appeared to me as though his forgiveness was never to be seen or given. I recall feelings of why he would not just let it go. Why does he still need to express such hatred and strong anger over every small event that happened years ago?

It could have been over cutting someone's grass, a lost baseball career or who someone else chose as a hunting partner. Heaven forbids, you wronged him, as he would talk about it for years to come especially if it was his own child who wronged him.

Holding forgiveness near and dear to his heart as he recalled each precious event with great detail and charged up energy time and time again. It was as if you could almost taste the disdain as he spoke. For only those who could prove to be worthy could attain and receive his precious forgiveness.

The purpose of digging into how I truly felt about forgiveness was not to slag my father but to gain a better understanding of where I stood with this process. Growing up I too had an exceptionally strong need to continue coveting this legacy as I held tight to the jewel of forgiveness which my 'unforgiver' obsessed over.

Not forgiving some days seemed to be a heavy cross to bear, while other times it seemed as if it was a badge of honour. Hoarding forgiveness, never using or spending it on anyone. After all, forgiveness is earned, and no one is really worthy of receiving it.

Unless you were my mother, she on the other hand seemed to have some sort of superhuman capacity to forgive and take whatever came her way. Maybe it was a combination of forgiveness and the coping skills of living with an alcoholic. Conditioning is all in itself due to the fact that most alcoholics seem to forget what they did when they were intoxicated.

It did not seem to matter how many times my father was drunk, hit her, or berated her with rude and hurtful comments she always seemed to forgive him. However, her ability to always push through that unpredictable onset of pain paid off for me, especially as a teenager. Sure, she may have seemed disappointed regarding my teenage choices and actions but not for exceedingly long, never to use previous events against me. Throughout my life, she has always been there for me in one form or another whether I noticed it or not.

Realising that in some sort of way, shape or form we all use people to best suit our needs with every thought, every word, and every action gaining some sort of payoff on many different levels. Also known as the human experience.

An experience in which I am not here to expose anyone, especially my parents but to work through the process of finding my own path and spark. *As* they too had to live and learn through years of their parent's negative conditioning. I truly feel my parents did and continue to do the best they can with the conditioning they too developed over their lifetime.

Hoping that in sharing this journey for what it is our minds will be open to change and open to forgiveness. As humans as we are always evolving and hopefully becoming more entuned beings with each generation.

Who knows? One day one of my children may even write a book about their lives sharing their own journey regarding our odd and unconventional parenting skills that may have driven them crazy as they work through their own negative conditioning that we have so graciously taught them.

"Challenge the voice from within who says you cannot do it." — Unknown.

As I explore the necessity for forgiveness, I am reminded of one-night many years ago. It had been early in my relationship dating my husband, Kevin. One evening I had been feeling tired, so I headed off to bed early. Less than an hour later Kevin quietly strolled into the room and proceeded to take his shirt off beside the bed. As he slowly pulled his shirt over his head, I let out what he described as the worst bloodcurdling scream, he had ever heard.

Later recalling he commented that it sounded as if someone was ripping my skin off as he frantically flicked on the light not sure what horrifying sight he would find. Simply to find me kneeling on the bed screaming bloody murder with all my skin still intact. However, even turning the light on did not wake me as the screaming continued. He quickly pounced onto the bed holding me tight as I came to my senses desperately reassuring me that everything was all right. 'It is just a bad dream,' he recited louder and louder until I came to. As my heartbeat pounded in my ears requiring many minutes to catch my breath or utter a single word.

'A bad dream!' I finally blurted out recalling each horrific detail I had just dreamt. 'What the fuck was that?' This was not similar to anything I had ever experienced before, so intense, and so real that I was sure the dark figure in my dream was going to kill me. 'What is happing to me? Was it something I just watched?' I reflect back to my evening which consisted of watching a sitcom and cuddling with Kevin on the couch. No scary shows, no late-night news broadcasts, nothing. I could not imagine what would have triggered this horrible and terrifying event. 'Is something wrong with me?' Recalling I had had many bad dreams growing up, but this was different.

The sheer realistic form of a dark shadowed person standing over me still sends shivers up my spine as my mind fired questions of needing to find an understanding as to why was this happening? And why *now* of all places? I had been feeling so content and comfortable with Kevin being part of my life. This left me unable to find any rational reason for this to be happening at this present time.

I proceeded to spend hours over the next few days reading about dreams and their meanings. As I researched into different dream states it shocked me with the vast difference in the definition between a nightmare and a night terror.

The term night terror was not something I had heard of prior to this experience. The medical definition describes a night terror as being a sleep disorder which initially floods me with denial as I have always been a person who loves sleep. It then listed all the specific characteristics which one may experience during a night terror.

I abruptly realise that what I experienced was indeed night terror as I made my way through the list. Anxiety episodes with extreme panic, check, often accompanied by screaming, check, flailing, check, fast breathing and sweating, check, and that usually occurs within a few hours after going to sleep, check.

Yep, that was exactly what it was as I noted that unresolved nightmares and trauma can result in night terrors which are labelled a sleeping disorder. Great, little did I know that these crazy night terrors would not be a rare occurrence and that I did indeed have a sleeping disorder.

The years passed and the night terrors frequently increased but noticeably came in a predictable cycle coinciding with trips to my hometown. Each time I decided to make the pilgrimage home to visit my family the night terrors would begin as the days got closer to our departure the frequency would increase.

Every few nights turned to every second night which escalated to every night right before leaving. I knew something was seriously wrong. However, understanding this connection did not remedy the night terror cycle from continuing with each upcoming visit. Nothing I did helped so as a last resort I decided that since these night terrors only occur when I go home, the solution was clear. I simply would not go home as often and our multiple trips home each year became less and less.

Shortly after Kevin and I got married we decided to move to Ontario, closer to his hometown. There we settled into our new jobs and a new house with big dreams of starting a new life and having a family of our very own.

Surely moving across Canada would help cure me of these ridiculous night terrors but no they still transpired. The only difference was the noticeable relief felt between each now rare visit. The night terrors became such a predictable event before each of our trips that I would just wake up now from my own scream or two totally annoyed that my sleep was being interrupted. My heart racing, sweating as if I had just run a marathon but so damn irritated with my now broken sleep pattern. It was almost comical as even Kevin would barely roll over to see if I am ok, most of the time not even-waking up.

As we arrived back home on one of our annual trips, we were greeted with the usual dysfunction in full force. My dad had been on one of his latest drinking binges and was acting like his usual gong-show self of unpredictable behaviour and rude condescending conversations. Alcohol has a special way of morphing one's memories into a twisted unbelievable story which the alcoholic swears to be true.

A memory in which my sister would be made the star villain, in her attempts to help safeguard my mom. Only to leave my poor sister to be the main target of his tantrums never to be forgiven over something perceived as being done.

During this visit, my sister and I sat around the campfire one night at her cottage chatting. I sensed she was upset as I began to dig into what was really bothering her. Realising the sheer stress and tension of being his target she then mentioned that she had been not sleeping well and had been experiencing night terrors.

What? You have them too? I was shocked and to my surprise, she tells me that along with her night terrors she reports that our two other sisters also suffer from these experiences. I could not believe it or could I? It did make perfect sense with all four of us growing up in the same household.

However, the real shocker was that mom too, had night terrors. 'Wait, did you just say that mom had them too? What is happening? For how long?' I can remember blurting out multiple questions as my mind spun so fast that it blurred my vision. Does that mean I could continue having these for thirty more years? Quickly realising that there would be no way in hell was I going to let that happen. In that moment I knew that as soon as Kevin and I got back to Ontario I was going to fix this even if it meant I was required to pay someone to help me.

Over the course of this short visit, my sister and I would delve into many conversations about these night terrors. The more we talked and shared the details of the actual night terrors the less isolated and alone I felt. However, there was something so weird and unexplainable one could not ignore the connection between all these people. Not only did we all experience night terrors, but we all seemed to have the exact same night terror of a blacked-out figure coming over our beds with the intention to kill us.

What did this mean? How is this possible? Why? Why did we all have the same night terror? As our conversations evolved, we chalked it up to living in the same family and having similar experiences which would appease me for now.

After we returned home to Ontario, I scoured google for days searching for something that could help me address these bizarre night terrors. Unlike most techniques, I had found many did not seem to work furthering my pursuit of digging around for inspirational tools and trying different techniques to cure myself.

I then came across quantum therapy which sounded interesting as I understood night terrors are formed around unresolved emotions from traumatic events. It was a technique which dealt with emotions trapped within past events which makes me stop to wonder if this could possibly work for me as I take a screenshot and continue searching for additional alternatives.

Funny enough after a conversation with a friend later that week, I explained that my back pain was acting up again, and she recommended I go see her osteopath. He specialized in many modalities such as acupuncture as well. She really liked him and highly recommended him, so I decided to give it a try. A few sessions in, I was progressing really well especially excited to be seeing some major improvements with my back. Not to mention enjoying the fact that he talked a lot about the energy flow within the body.

Energy flow, universe and one-ness was not something I heard many people discuss outside of a few close family members and friends, so I found this to be extremely refreshing. After a few treatments, my progress started to plateau and during one of my treatment sessions, he asked me why I thought my back had not improved beyond a certain point. We then had a very frank and open conversation about trapped emotions. Emotions that I thought might be trapped in my back.

He then asked me if I had heard of quantum therapy. That's a weird coincidence, I thought I had just come across it during one of my google searches a few weeks back. As I told him about my search he just grinned and said that his wife who unbeknownst to me also worked in his clinic and specialized in quantum therapy sessions. I knew at that moment feeling a spark that the universe was giving me a sign, a sign which demanded to be acted on.

He then stepped out of the room, only to return a moment later with his wife for a quick introduction. She quickly explained that quantum therapy was one of those steppingstones to help deal with past traumas. More so the trapped emotion than the specific details of an event. Trapped emotions that you had the ability to release and that the specific number of emotions released would depend on how open or willing my mind would be to release them. She also explained that the session could take upwards of four hours to complete.

Interesting. I would be able to feel and sense the release of a trapped emotion. Curious, I stood there saying nothing of my night terrors or that I was already interested in coming for a session. I just smiled and said I would think about it.

Making my way to the receptionist's desk to pay for my session doubt started to set in. Do I want my osteopath's wife to know all about my messy past? Do I even want to rehash everything from the past that I have worked so hard on overcoming? The receptionist handed me my recipe along with a brochure. Smiling an unusual smile and saying nothing feeling weird I glanced down realising it was a brochure for Quantum Therapy.

Ok Universe! I am listening and acknowledge that this may be the method and time to deal with these ridiculous night terrors once and for all. Sensing the yearning to heal myself.

On my drive home from my appointment, the excuses started to roll in pretty hard causing me to question if I could handle all the emotions that a session like this may bring about. Fear of the unknown lead to fear of what kind of seriously fucked up emotions these night terrors must be hiding. Which fuelled the fear of wasting my money on something that may not even help due to the sheer cost.

That evening, I gave Kevin a quick and basic explanation of what just happened at my appointment of how quantum therapy sort of worked based on what little knowledge I had of this technique. I could feel his energy rise at the prospect of me overcoming these night terrors.

Instead of matching his excitement I choose to inject the conversation with all of my fears regarding cost and ability to complete this session. Lastly, mentioning that there might be a slight chance that quantum therapy could, maybe, possibly, but not for sure, with no guarantees, may be able to help with my night terrors.

Without hesitation. He blurted out. So, when are you booking it?

His answer took me by surprise but not sure why after all he had been the one sleeping next to me all those nights through all those night terrors. With me screaming bloody murder in the night it had never dawned on me how this must have felt to experience a loved one having a night terror. His overwhelming feelings of helplessness and worry for my well-being were followed by his natural loving instincts of wanting to help me.

I explained that I wanted to sleep on it because it was a lot of money to spend especially on myself since currently there had been zero dollars spent or invested in my own mental health. I had no problem buying a new table, gym membership, play structure for the kids or any practical purchases that the whole family will be using never contemplating twice about it. On the other hand, spending any sort of money on myself for mental wellness was a totally foreign concept to me.

As I voiced all my concerns to Kevin, he just calmly commented that it is the perfect time to try something new and not to worry about spending the money as it would be worth it just to try.

Eventually, all my excuses as to why quantum therapy would be not a good fit for me faded as the spark of hope started to return. I scheduled an appointment, and we met the next week. I took the day off and proceeded to my appointment. Booking it first thing in the morning because I knew if my session were booked for any later in the day, I would have spent half of the day stressing over it or worst not even showing up as I made up some lame excuse as to why I needed to cancel.

I arrive at my session scared shitless but still hoping for a Christmas miracle. I take a seat and she began to explain that we would *not* be dredging up specific events. What? Really. OK, I am pretty excited now sensing my mind release and open to the possibilities. As we work our way through the session, she continues to explain we are just going to identify specific feelings and emotions tied to specific people. Emotions that were trapped causing disharmony in the body. This quantum therapy session was unlike anything I had experienced before. The very act of accessing trapped emotions associated with each person was unreal.

Unexpected people and emotions popped up affirming that it was not about the details of the actual events at all. It was more about the strongest emotions I felt towards each person.

It was life changing as she had opened my eyes up to a whole new world of forgiveness. A world of forgiveness that had nothing to do with the other person and everything to do with myself, just me. Me and my feelings. Trapped feelings that I had for that person and even for myself and through the openness and willingness to see the emotion for what it was I could then release it.

The four hours flew by as if it had only been thirty minutes. Closing out the session, I felt a neutral calmness pour over me until she proposed I make one simple decision that I knew fuelled these night terrors. A simple choice of making the pilgrimage back home or choosing yourself.

Going back home would inevitably give my power away whereas deciding to skip a year and make a stand for myself had the ability to release the trauma fuelling these night terrors. The therapist then reassured me that this one big decision to choose myself would allow me the time, energy, and power I essentially required to heal.

Arriving home from my appointment I went directly to the phone ringing up each family member reporting that we were not coming home for an annual trip this year. Damn, it felt so scary and so great at the same time realising that cancelling our annual trip would allow for a huge shift. A shift in creating a powerful space for lasting healing.

The power to choose forgiveness for others allowed me to heal myself. Happily reporting that by then I did finally return home three years later without one episode, I continue to this day to be night terror free.

"Forgiveness is the essential gift we can choose to give or not to give to ourselves." – Jennifer Aves

Forgiveness has come to me in many phases throughout my life especially over the past few months as I recall just how powerful this single quantum therapy session was. A session that changed the way I viewed forgiveness forever. It has become such an integral part of my life as I document my journey paying my eternal gratitude to myself for embracing this once seemingly impossible task.

Yes, you can Jen, you can forgive. Thank you. Thank you. Thank you.

It is big. Big, and bold, literally, and figuratively so big that I felt it really required to shout out all on its own. I remind myself of that pivotal quantum therapy session where forgiveness truly focused on me and not the other person. I realised today that I had lost sight of what forgiveness represented as a gift given to oneself.

A gift with an unlimited supply for personal growth to be tapped into and yes, this may resemble a hallmark card which by the way, I would seriously recommend you buy for yourself. To hold and reflect on when needed as it is the one gift that not only saved me from my 'non-forgiver' self but help super-size me into starting to become an ever-evolving version of myself as forgiveness is a choice.

During one's life forgiveness can be necessary for heavy emotions and light emotions as this gesture holding tight to charged emotions for so many people. Memories which are painful and sometimes almost unbelievable as horrific events can seem unfathomable to the thoughts of forgiveness if not impossible. As I ventured out on my own looking for ways to take back my spark, I made sure to take my time with forgiveness. I started with small emotional events and worked my way up with baby steps. Baby stepping my way as I take time to work through all the trapped emotions with numerous trials and errors. I knew I could achieve forgiveness regarding most people in my life on my own, but not all people.

If forgiveness is all about me, it is not a gift that I am required to give to the other person. It is the gift that I would give to myself. An exchange of sorts of willingness to let go and receive. The giving up of an incessant need of carrying the hurt and resentment in exchange that I would receive a greater gift. The gift of peace of mind, just for me and not the other person.

Clearly understanding that forgiveness is by no means saying that whatever the other person did is right or ok.

Quite the contrary the reasons for why a person did what they do, really does not matter as most of the time we will never know why. However, let us say I did know why they did what they did; would that make the event any less painful, probably not.

It was blowing my mind to realise that it was truly all about me and not the other person who wronged me if I was just willing to let go. Letting go of the resentment gifted me with peace of mind that possessed a far greater power than any amount of anger, pain, or resentment. Essentially letting go of the rat race in the mind of all the whys. Why did they do that? Why did this happen to me? Why did they act that way? Why did they say that? Why? Why? Why?

Delving into forgiveness exposed how past conditioning was tainting new adventures with past experiences. Old mindsets love to reinforce the idea that there is no such thing as forgive and forget that forgiving was somehow letting the offender off the hook. Weird enough I did forget, OK maybe not fully forgotten but I was able to stop the 'non-forgiver' from exhausting my life with flashbacks of the past as it consumed my mind with all the why's. By starving the 'non-forgiver' of energy it allowed past emotions to be much less charged, almost rendering them neutral in a sense.

My two cents when delving into forgiveness you are likely going to examine your relationship with those that brought you up. Those who raised you, loved and cared for you, even those who hurt or neglected you. Forgiveness around my childhood was definitely a process but one that literally saved me as it began by examining the way I viewed my parents. Realising that we all mirror our past conditioning, traumatic situations experienced, and a shit ton of choices made along the way.

This point of view now allowed me to have a fresh perspective on my past as I no longer felt upset or sad for my mother for staying with an alcoholic all these years. For it was her life path that has helped shape me into the person I am today. A person who is no longer fuelled by judging someone else's journey. With these new lenses of looking at my parents with an open mind, it started to bring about a new perspective of my parents due to the fact that I was no longer hyper-focused on how they wronged me but what went right. I began to see the more humorous side of my parents as our conversations became lighter even experiencing gratitude at the end of a phone conversation instead of disappointment.

The love and forgiveness for both of my parents is forever ongoing. The longer I stayed true to my path of figuring shit out for myself the more I forgave the past and picked up the pieces of myself that I had left behind. After all, parents only know what they too have been conditioned to learn. As many grew up in a generation of fear and intimidation with little to no positive examples of growth it is very likely that they will pass those traits on.

Thankfully, a conscious shift in parenting has taken place. A respect for all, the child, the mother, the father, the entire family and beyond, no matter who makes up your family circle. Thank God for forgiveness as becoming a parent has opened my eyes up to the essential need for it otherwise, we would all be screwed. This is an essential need for family dynamics and flow as we are continually and hopefully learning from our mistakes. As a parent, I have come to quickly realise that there is no manual, no certification or the exact right way to achieve a balanced home life.

Reminding myself as a parent that we are not given any fancy course to best show you how to teach and handle our children. Or what to do when their behaviour is driving us crazy as the only guideline, we are given is the example we grew up with. As some of you following this journey may have now reflected back on how you grew up and are demanding a refund! Please know that you too are enough, just the way you are.

Except for a rare few who received that upgraded parenting course from their parents. We mirror our parents' parenting style. Or we attempt to do the complete opposite with varied success. Therefore, if you have evolved your parenting from the one you have been conditioned with, I applaud you for wanting more as this took reprogramming your past conditioning.

Forgiveness has also exposed that as a parent I do not know everything, and we do not have all the answers. Frankly, most of the time we are just winging it in hopes to not totally screw up our kids by the end of it. Even in all the chaos of growing up, it became abundantly clear to me now as a parent that we are all doing the best we can with the knowledge we have alongside all of the choices we are willing to make. This acknowledgement that we have a choice each time we implement and use our parental persuasion making micro choices throughout our day which will influence the paths of our children.

No pressure just the sheer outcome of these two little souls depending on me to guide them. Well, guess what kids, parents do not have all the answers. We say the wrong things, do the wrong things and act the wrong way. In this realization, that we too, the same as our children are learning and growing along the way. Also, leads me to 'the holy shit neither did my parents' moment as my dad grew up with an alcoholic parent who ruled with an iron fist so the odds were fairly good by example that he would turn out exactly the way he did. His generation did not have any talk of positive parenting, oneness, self-help podcasts or YouTube meditations, instead, they had alcohol and sex. Resonating and understanding this perspective allowed me to let it go, to forgive them and to continue to forgive them.

"Forgiving others opens your heart to start the learning process of how to forgive yourself."

— Jennifer Aves

Understanding that in the grand scope of a lifetime, we have extraordinarily little time to teach a child. Which in hindsight is probably a good thing as with a shorter timeline the odds are slimmer that we would totally screw them up for life. A small window to raise them and get them ready to venture out on their own, is one of the most stressful and yet more satisfying jobs I have ever experienced.

It has taken me some major mind resets to be willing to let go of the past along with embracing some kick-ass tools to achieve a comfortable flow around forgiveness. Knowing that I have progressed with forgiving others around me, my kids, my husband, my parents basically, forgiving everyone who was in my life except for one.

One especially important person, me!

As I finished up documenting my journey this far, I realised that within all of these words I have never really addressed forgiving myself. I knew that forgiveness of myself was at the core of this gripping sadness and would not only help myself but ultimately everyone else would feel this positive ripple. Acknowledging that forgiving myself was scary as hell but non the less a big deal.

At this point, things were starting to change as forgiveness of others started to effortlessly role out taking on a life of its own almost as if it had an essential need to evolve my personal growth allowing me to then shed many trapped emotions. This essential need to forgive others became a vital part of each day much like the essential need to breathe and drink water. Now if only I felt this willingness and drive to forgive myself this freely.

Reality check-in: Day 120

Mind check-in:

Forgiveness for myself. Not sure what to say about that.

Body check-in:

Gym is closed trying to get out for walks. Feeling really tired lately.

Spiritual check-in:

Feel like a weight has lifted when thinking of my past.

CHAPTER 8

Never underestimate the power of a good poop

If you do not enjoy potty humour you may want to skip ahead to the next page although if you were not offended by my shitty attitude or essential need to be a people pleaser, we must be good.

So yes, I said it, never underestimate the power of a good poop. Gross right, but so good at the same time. As the days tick by into my year of healing, I have not only released most of my shitty mindsets but loosened the grip of sadness. As I feel the pressure to let go understanding that up to now, I had been choosing the hard way in life.

Letting it build up over the years constipating me with fear, anger, resentment, and sadness with unrealistic ideals of trying to be the perfect person in the eyes of others. Blocking everyone out , reeking of my shitty attitude. Until that fateful day that I started to relax and choose to let go, let go of all the shitty preconceived ideas and conditioning that I had held onto for so many years. These endless years of conditioning, resulting in me only wanting one thing. The single act to purge out everything. The purge of old mindsets, a purge of old thought patterns and specifically to purge all these old, trapped emotions. Emotions that were holding me back of letting go of the resentment, letting go of the guilt, letting go of the fear and most importantly letting go of the sadness.

Working my way through all these stuck emotions, flushing them away from my mind, body, and spirit forever. The sheer act of letting go became so satisfying and necessary with each day.

Similar to breathing and yes pooping as this was an essential full system purge in order to move forward to new and improved me.

So, you're welcome, I tried to use as many poopy puns as possible after all, if you are going to document your journey for all to see and admit to the world you have a shitty attitude you may as embrace the child in you and have fun with it.

Reality check-in: Day 130
Mind check-in:
Working my way through forgiveness. Forgiving myself is the hardest task yet but it seems to bring the most amount of growth.

Body check-in:
A rollercoaster of super tired and exhausted to energetic and productive.

Spiritual check-in:
Major growth happening, feeling more connected than ever.

A purge is to rid someone or something of an unwanted quality, condition or feeling which sounded accurate as I endeavoured through this journey of forgiving myself.

I find myself not being motivated this month to share my journey as I slowly become consumed by the covid fog.

Ashamed as I finally admit to myself that I had been on such a high of self-growth only to be pulled under by covid. This part of my journey was by far the most pungent and gross thing I have had to work through. I began to feel so drained and out of control as my emotions and thoughts started to run wild.

It left me little to no choice but to stop and examine how and what I thought of myself. Was it me or my environment that required to be purged? Or was it both? Who knows, but what I did know was that it was time to purge myself of all the unwanted qualities, years of conditioning and negative feelings that I was harbouring within. Time to create an environment that allowed me to heal even during a pandemic.

Currently, Covid was consuming much of my day I could not even turn the radio on while I was making dinner without crying and going into a negative tailspin with their every word. As I scoured the internet the constant talk of death and the demand of safety precautions reinforced my obsessive incessant need to track and follow the rising death toll.

I started to notice the sheer impact of Covid even as I lay in bed at night as it crept into the recapping of gratitude for the day. Every night began in the same manner I am so grateful for my family being safe and not having Covid. Which is not a bad thing other than the fact that this was the one and only thing that I was grateful for. Finding something to be positive about was becoming an overwhelming challenge. Not because there was nothing to be grateful for, far from it.

There was plenty to be grateful for even Covid, in the beginning, brought me a sense of peace and gratitude for my health and life. Only now this focus has left made me numb frozen in time. Whether I liked it or not I was living through a once in lifetime world chaotic experience. It was something so new, so scary, so unbelievable, and so life changing. Humanity as a whole was becoming a part of history, a history which would be documented and studied for generations to come.

As covid started to escalate it began to linger around me creating its own friction as the underlying messages tainted each day. I admit there is a need to educate and inform oneself about what is happening in the world whether you want to believe in it or not. As large numbers of people were dying and covid had aggressively popped my positive little bubble that day in the grocery store.

Leaving the incessant news to ring in my ears as it surrounded me in a thick dense fog as the days passed. It was ever-present, at work, on the radio, on social media even at home most conversations resulted in the topic of covid being discussed. As it crept its way into every conversation with despair, disbelief, and heartbreak for the sheer number of people who were affected by covid's impact. Effecting society, the economy, one's home, family, job and essentially life as we knew it. Therefore, what could one do to help themselves? Apparently, nothing but stand still, helplessly unable to move forward.

As the thick fog of Covid made its way into our home the unbearable deafening noise constantly boomed sounds of metal-on-metal smashing around me unannounced. Covid was creating a severe traffic jam of chaos as the fog seemed to blind society with casualties at every corner. The largest traffic jam, the world as a whole had experienced in my lifetime. I undoubtedly have heard of other catastrophes in my lifetime however, the only difference was that past events never personally affected me nor well affected the whole world. This catastrophic event was different simply because it was the only catastrophic event that affected me personally. It would affect me and everyone else on this planet on a very personal and real scale. A much grander scale that could and would not be ignored even if you wanted to. The sheer rapid rate of this fog had the power to bring the world to a catastrophic stop as the densely thick fog settled into what little space was left I had no choice but to notice as I started to address forgiveness from within as this fog, some days impacted me with serious and instant impact leaving me completely dazed, lost and paralyzed by fear.

We were all being forced to stop whether we admitted it or not in order to take notice of one's life. Not noticing anyone but myself in this fog as it triggered many questions. How had it impacted me? How had it affected my day-to-day life? What precious things I could no longer do? Pretty much me, me, me, me, stuck without the ability to seek a way out of this chaotic foggy traffic jam. I spent much of the time wallowing in self-pity and negative thoughts resulting in feelings of being paranoid, helpless, and weak. Absolutely consumed by fear of the deafening noise of Covid that surrounded me.

The longer I stood frozen in the covid fog the longer I began to tire of standing still almost as if frozen in time. I closed my eyes and tried to bring myself back to this very moment realising how consumed I was becoming with each day that passed as I listened to Covid stats, thought about Covid, read about Covid, and talked about Covid. Being aware that I was indeed stuck in the fog was essential as a first step in making my way out of it. I began to notice something between each deafening crash of Covid, a quiet little sound appeared as if it was calling to me. I squeezed my eyes closed and tried to concentrate on what I was hearing. There it was again, something so familiar and so faint. Between the deafening crashes of emotional self-pity, I felt my spirit demanding change. 'Be here now,' but how? I could hear deep within that small voice of my spirit calling out to me. You got this, just breathe, please open your eyes and wake up.

The dense thick fog around me started to part ever so slightly as I found myself standing on the open road resembling a deer frozen and staring directly into the headlights, stunned realising it is about to get run over. Not sure if I would have the energy or courage to move after sensing where I was and what was about to happen if I did not move. At, that very moment I seem to be frozen as a victim of circumstance only wanting to be alive choosing at that last split second to help myself ignite a spark from within. Lighting up the perfect opening to a path to safety I decided to make a break for it. Exhausted from being frozen and paralyzed with fear I wearily pivot, bobbing, and weaving away from the oncoming traffic which does not even notice my presence as they are on their own mission to clear the traffic jam. I bolt to the side of the busy traffic-jammed freeway heading straight into the forest looking for safety and some sort of peace. Exhausted, I collapse onto the ground as I finally make it to safety as I lay there for days from sheer mental exhaustion.

As my energy returns, self-reflection kicked in as it triggered a roller coaster of questions and emotions. What was I spending my time on? What was I thinking about? When were my negative thoughts? What inspires me? What needed to be purged? Was my day spent in love, joy, and creativity? No, no and definitely not, now overwhelmed by the sheer number of questions that needed to be assessed with so many choices to be had I froze. Lying there I began questioning my timing to assess these issues as doubts of my decision to veer off the main road rushed in. After all, we were in the midst of a bloody pandemic. As the questions finished flooding in, I realised that my eyes were still fixed back on the sliver of the freeway I could see through the trees with flashing billboards of death toll states attempting to pull me back in. I took in a deep breath, closed my eyes, and allowed silence to take over as my spirit quickly realised it had its moment to be heard. 'You got this! One thing at a time, please come back to this very moment', as it plants a seed of reassurance that things would be OK.

As I lay there feeling the warmth of the earth on my skin content with the recovery time, I had taken to reconnect a tender flood of heat engulfed my chest. As the warmth sparked my inner strength, I made my way back up to my feet feeling my legs rooting themselves in the positive energy of nature. Searching the horizon with my eyes for guidance and strength determined this time to find my path. A path of determination to avoid the busy road consumed with the fog of covid promising myself to reconnect with this beautiful path through the forest if I ever strayed again. Knowing that the thick fog on the busy road would always exist, always present running parallel along this beautiful forest with many paths that led back to many choices. With each choice I acknowledge that it had the ability to lead me back to that traffic jam, however, knowing it also only took one choice to make my way back to this beautiful path no matter where I was.

"Who and what we surround ourselves with is who and what we become. In the midst of good people, it is easy to be good. in the midst of bad people, it is easy to be bad".

— Karen Marie Moning.

How does one stay on this path within all of this chaos and what would I choose to be my story? This would be the burning question. I could have easily stayed on that road branding this as the worst part of my life allowing Covid to consume me with stress and sadness. Or I could choose this to be a life-changing period of personal growth as I took the opportunity to share my self-growth journey in spite of covid life trying to rear its ugly head and attempting to distract me from my purpose.

As I stared right into this chaotic situation it proved that self-growth was indeed possible in any circumstance. A choice between allowing Covid to consume me with an innate ability to pull me into a spiralling pit of despair and self-pity or would it help motivate and propel me to something greater? The thing is, honestly, I would come to choose both paths with many good days followed by covid entranced days. Some true inspiration mixed with spiralling sadness and self-pity as I acknowledged that these emotions are what being human is all about as I choose just how long I am willing to endure the traffic jam.

And so... the purge began.

The process of totally shutting myself off from all social media and the news. I asked my husband, Kevin to inform me if any earth-shattering events occurred otherwise, I did not need to hear about it. I no longer checked the daily rising death toll or who was in the running to create the first vaccine or heaven forbid what was happening with the USA's political gong show. Not to mention the many theories of how, what, and why Covid existed as Facebook got flooded with conspiracies and anti-mask articles. Only giving my attention to assess what we could do in this very moment by wearing a mask and social distance as I refused to give into the hysteria over what I could not change. Encouraging my mind to return to gratitude whenever needed and as often as needed as I attempted to figure out a way to teach myself how in the midst of all this chaos, could one find gratitude.

This purge would be the first step that I needed in order to shift my attention to positive thoughts, words, and actions. An integral step of purging myself of this negative social feed gave my mind and spirit some space to breathe relaxing back into the present moment. In creating this moment something amazing sparked, it was a pure spark of hope. Hope of doing something positive as I revelled in the positive energy washing over me.

"Life does not come with a remote. Get up and change it yourself." — Unknown

Tonight, my husband Kevin and I sat around the kitchen table discussing ways to make a positive impact as we attempt to turn the chaos of Covid into a purpose. As I glance across the table while he speaks, I sense his energy shift as his face lights up it reminds me just how much I missed sitting around the table talking and enjoying one another's company. We began tossing around ideas of how one goes about creating a positive impact all the while laughing and enjoying our brainstorming session.

Our focus was to keep it simple. We were on a mission to find a fun little project. A project that would be enjoyable for us to do together with a positive twist. Do we create something, make something, buy something, or sell something? We kept returning back to the basic concept that it needed to be simple as negative talk of Covid tried to interrupt our beautiful conversation we would just squash it with realizations that something positive had to come from all this friction and negativity.

Discussing how if Covid did not happen, would we have felt such a strong need to do something positive for ourselves and others, probably not. Somehow this need for positive change started to outweigh the daunting pressures of Covid. A need to make some kind of positive impact, even if some days it was just for our own sanity. As we delved into all the particulars of what? Where? How? The hardest question that needed to be answered was, how could we make a positive impact and have fun creating it all at the same time.

A range of ideas flew onto the paper from the inspiring and energizing to the silly and downright ridiculous ideas. We talked and laughed about all the things that were currently inspiring us. It all seemed to come back to the same thing, Audible books, Podcasts, Movies, YouTube, Music, Facebook, and Instagram. Damn!!! Damn you, social media. Why did all of our ideas of inspiration always take us back to some sort of social media? I just finished purging myself of it, however, Kevin reassures me this time it could and would be different. If we kept our mission simple and pure. Do something positive and loving that creates a positive ripple. He then went on to explain that this is and could be a simple process of surrounding ourselves in a positive environment, so that is exactly what we did.

Unfollowed, unfriended, and deleted all things negatively feeding our poisonous mindsets on social media. It became my mission of making any social media platform I was on full of inspiration and positive energy. To my surprise, the internet on all platforms were loaded. Beyond my wildest expectations. I could not believe how many years I had spent on the negative roller coaster of social media. Now, all it took was asking myself this one simple test question to guide me.

How do I feel? Each time I listened to or spoke to anyone, I applied this test question. If I felt miserable, negative, or worse sad, I knew I was not spending my precious time and energy on anything positive. Deleting and unfollowing creating the perfect space for growth and reflection. If I got off my phone or finished a conversation and felt inspired, happy, grateful, or energized I knew I had made the right choices to create a positive environment for myself. Reminding myself making sure to thank them and the universe for taking the time to connect with each other. This simple question worked its' magic for my downtime if I decided to go on my phone which is why we felt confident that if we decided to create something on social media, it was going to be on our terms and in our own positive way.

Reality check-in: Day 138

Mind check-in:

My attitude adjustment is going well, better than expected.

Body check-in:

Noticed I too have put on Covid pounds, which needs to be addressed. Realising I may be addicted to the snooze button.

Spirit check-in:

Feeling more content in quiet moments. Excited to look for opportunities for random acts of kindness.

As my phone vibrates lighting up on the table my good friend, Anne texted me that she was out for a run and could I come out onto the deck for a quick visit. I called down to the kids that Anne and her girls were stopping by for a quick driveway visit after online school.

Social distancing was a new and foreign concept which held its challenges. As she arrived, I popped out onto the patio proceeding to the railing overlooking the driveway. I spot Anne she was alone as my daughter, Makayla, who was now at my heels excited to see the girls even if it was for a quick visit from afar for just a moment. Right away she saw that Anne was alone and shot me the death stare as she high tailed it quickly back into the house making me take a mental note to go back in and check on her when I was done. As soon as I looked at Anne, she burst into tears killing me not to run down and put my arms around her.

Currently, we have been social distancing and having driveway visits when we can squeeze them in as she is a nurse at our local hospital. A nurse who has been screening people at the Covid door as well as working the Covid tent. Anne is not upset about having to screen people however, she is devastated because last week she had to send her two girls to their grandmother's house to live because she was so frightened of getting them sick.

Even after making sure all the precautions were taken of showering and changing her clothes. Things were getting intense at the hospital and after spending four twelve-hour shifts in a row and feeling like she could no longer keep her family safe it left her no other option but to drop them off. I could not imagine being separated from my kids as my heart sank with each of her tears.

Recalling our plan shared that if someone in either of our homes got COVID a few weeks prior if the shit hit the fan. I could not believe that the shit had hit the fan.

After thirty minutes of us standing out in the rain both now crying, consoling her, and her me attempting to cheer up each other and ourselves by getting a few laughs in as good friends always do. I went inside straight to the bathroom and cried after splashing my face with cold water, I went downstairs to check on Makayla.

She barked at me in a pissed-off voice, 'Where are the girls?' Forgetting that when Anne-sent me the text, I had yelled down to the kids to come up for a quick visit. I presumed the girls were out for a run with her because they were always where with her. I then explained that they were at their grandmother's and that they may be there for a while. Makayla then started screaming that she hated this whole thing as she slammed her bedroom door.

Covid has brought many difficult emotions up: feelings of fear, anger, and resentment for all of us. This has definitely been a trying time as we ride the emotional rollercoaster that could be felt by all however in all of this chaos it would also be a time of obvious gratefulness. Gratefulness for being healthy, grateful for being safe, having our jobs, working from home while our kids did online schooling and grateful for being alive.

I was in a constant state of growth looking for ways to make sure we were not trapping any crazy emotions, especially Covid emotions. Remembering a while back in one of my many searches for help when releasing emotions, I had discovered the power of emotion in the book, *The Emotion Code*.

A great tool to help understand the range of emotions and techniques to help move through and deal with negative emotions. It also started to allow me to get to know myself better and to release trapped negative energy and emotions.

When I first discovered this method, I would have never guessed I would be using it years later for Covid as I engaged my whole family in mini emotion-clearing sessions later that weekend. We all began to see a shift. Do not get me wrong. Anger, fear, and frustration still surfaced, but not as frequent and not as wild.

CHAPTER 9

Is there more than one way to peel and eat a banana?

Yes, one would most definitely agree that there is more than one way to peel and eat a banana. Most times it is almost comical watching someone peel and eat this phallic fruit as we too have had many jokes fly around our house with good friends over someone eating a banana.

Watching the hilarious, ridiculous, and sometimes even sensual techniques we have adapted. Peeling it from the top, peel from the bottom as some fully peel the coveted banana breaking off tiny pieces or the ultimate decision of does one bring the banana to their head or their head to the banana.

The funny thing with all this banana business is that none of it really matters. The only simple fact that truly counts is that we are all individuals. Individuals who complete tasks in life with a slightly different manner and technique. Right down to the simplest of tasks similar to peeling and eating a banana. Resulting in all, with the same outcome of banana being peeled and eaten, but like all humans we are conditioned to judge each other's every move.

Therefore please, peel and eat that damn banana anyway that pleases you because sometimes this observation comes with joy and laughter while other times it comes with judgement and negativity. Sometimes positive energy is created from the simplest of actions while we enjoy a mutual laugh over a style of eating a banana resulting in a positive energy flow. While other times we judge and criticize others allowing the negative criticism of over analysing people's actions in every way shape and form.

As we analyse, observe and judge these are vital components that play a role in our survivor mechanism. A mechanism for analysing and protecting us from dangerous situations. However, in today's world, we are unlikely to be hunted by wild animals looking to us to be their next meal. We are more likely looking to hunt down other humans or sadly be hunted. As the ego picks apart our every move as it makes sure to voice its strong opinions on what would have been the better method.

We all know the ego loves a big juicy human as a meal consuming it with judgement and the expectation for others to somehow know and do everything the exact same way that we do is ridiculous if not impossible. This unrealistic expectation is a product of our conditioning, a conditioning which makes us believe we are experts in all things with one right way to accomplish the task at hand. Living a life of my way or the highway. Never acknowledging the sheer creativity of people and the infinite possibility of different ways to complete a task or even peel and eat a banana. With the ridiculous notion of how someone else should complete a task when we ourselves have never experienced that task at hand. Going into great detail of how we would know and master this task in a specific way if we too just had that same banana to peel and eat ourselves.

As I sit down to document this part of my journey it has brought to my attention my own judgement of other's peeling and banana-eating techniques. Realising that I too had a bad habit of expecting those around me, especially my husband and kids to peel that damn banana exactly the way I do and wanted, exactly how fast I wanted in the exact time frame that I needed.

Heaven forbids, you do not pick up that damn banana and peel it without hesitation, it would send me through the roof. Metaphorically speaking, of course, I had little to no patience or realization that people will always follow their own individual way in their own time frame to complete a task.

Demands and expectations which had a way of cycling through my mind and weaselling their way right down to the smallest of tasks. Why did they do that? What is taking so long? Why aren't they done yet? I would have done it like this, this is a much simpler way, Blah! Blah! Blah!

Thankfully, for their sake, my understanding and realization were expanding each day that passed as I evaluated the way I look at each situation as it is ever-changing with the ability to affect a positive shift.

This realization of my expectation of myself and others caused for reflection each time my shitty attitude appeared. Acknowledging that it is always going to be about growth and learning and not necessarily about getting something perfectly right. Realising that sometimes I have been a jerk to my family was not that big of a surprise since I started down this journey of realization. A journey that has allowed me to become less judgemental of others and myself. The initial extremely uncomfortable mindset of this realization soon began to wear off as I admitted to myself that negativity and judgement were conditioned into my everyday behaviours.

For example, this morning begins with a bang as I blurt out, 'Please empty the dishwasher, I already asked you to do to empty it *three times*! Hurry up!'

Thoughts of how I could have already emptied this damn dishwasher ten times over and how long is it going to take these kids to establish a habit engulfed my mind. I did include the word please in my demand after all, therefore me screaming could not be that bad justifying my negative behaviour.

Unknowingly releasing my shitty attitude before I could stop her from digging her heels in as she readied to unleash her furry. I stop and take a moment to create space as I notice the weight and tension lingering in the air and slowly making its way across my chest. Seeing that it has been less than one minute from my first request which was also barked at the kids so no wonder no one came running. I agree that asking your kids to empty the dishwasher is never a negative as it gives them responsibilities and a sense of pride for contributing to their household. However, I found that most of the time when I had little to no patience and snapped that it was rarely about what I was asking them to do. More so it was about how I asked them.

As my mind made space and I took a few moments to detach from this current situation to ask myself what I was so afraid of.

Remembering that addressing fear could catapult growth with this one simple question of 'what am I so afraid of?'. Almost every time when it came to dealing with my kids and me losing my patience the fear of looking like a bad mother would surface. As if in some way a lack of emptying the dishwasher would make them ill-prepared for life resulting in everyone saying that their mother must not have taught them how to be responsible. Shedding light on how much importance I put on what others may perceive of the quality of my parenting skills demonstrating my own lack of self-worth once again.

The presence of this realization of fear allowed me to bring myself back to the present moment. Does it truly matter that the dishes are still in the dishwasher? The world will probably not end if the dishwasher is emptied later bringing about gratitude and knowing that I am a good mother who is doing the best she can with the knowledge she has at this present moment.

A rush of genuine love for my children made for a quick emotional resolution and after a few moments of clarity, I heard them creep their way up the stairs to see if the coast was clear. I then followed up with a heartfelt apology and we all openly made fun of my adult-size tantrum.

The result of addressing my own judgement has noticeably allowed for a quicker correction and an ability to apologize for my shitty attitude which has positively impacted our kids as we notice them rapidly shift their own words, thoughts, and actions.

"You don't attract what you want. You attract what you are." — Wayne Dyer

Lately, I have begun to notice many signs from the universe. A sign can be an object, quality, event, or entity whose presence or occurrence indicates something else to come. It is funny how the universe will present new opportunities many times, and in many ways. The universe patiently waiting for me to take advantage of a new opportunity as I am beginning to notice that these signs usually came in the form of repetition.

The repetition of numbers, names, books, people, and the list goes on and on. Realising that the universe is always in a constant state of energetic exchange with like attracting like. Therefore, understanding that if I am in a negative mood and mindset, then negative things will come my way. Similar to a positive mindset attracting positive circumstances almost as if the universe is throwing me breadcrumbs to see if I will follow along to a more positive path. A path I have dreamt up for myself and now just needed to trust that it already existed, however, testing to see if I am hungry enough to follow the breadcrumbs to something new.

Tonight, started like most evenings curled up on the couch with my laptop and as I started to type away our dog Fozzie relentlessly tries to climb all over my laptop. Usually, I stop and give him a little love only to have him go on his merry way but tonight I pushed him away time after time. With one final attempt he scurried across my legs and chewed my toes, I giggle causing him to quickly pounce spastically licking my face while he crushes every key on my keyboard spraying a barrage of letters onto my word document.

My first emotion was anger as I shoved him down off of my laptop questioning how could he ruin and interrupt my important work? Catching myself I stop to breathe in and try to observe my behaviour without judgement. In the past, this would have been the perfect excuse to stop what I was doing resulting in me spending the remainder of the evening in a bad mood complaining to my husband about the dog's poor behaviour and how he should fix it.

Thankfully not this time as the action of stopping to take that simple pause to create space steps in. A pause that I value as it allows space and time to connect as it brings me back into this present moment.

Piquing my interest as to what sign the universe is trying to tell me, I begin to relax into the moment. Questioning if it was to use friction as inspiration or maybe just the simple fact that there is always time to stop and pet the puppy or smell the roses.

A task that in the past I gave little to no value in, often feelings of being too busy or at least perceived thoughts that I was too busy to stop to enjoy the simple things in life such as petting our puppy. As I sit and open myself up to the gratitude of the universe and Fozzie for being that playful, energetic spirit as he is reminding me that in life even when you are working, you have a choice. A choice to fill your time with fun, energy, and laughter or a choice to fill it with excuses, urgency, chaos, blame and negativity.

'KEY RESET.'
Blah work! Today, I am in dire need of a reset.

It seems to be one of those days. A day where my patience and compassion for myself and others are wearing thin. Very thin. I could literally hear my mind slammed shut. I was totally frustrated with my current task list at hand leaving me wishing I had taken the day off or possibly looking for a new career.

I remind myself of all the tools I have at my disposal to push through these uncomfortable times. As working from home loved to challenge my attitude as it even impacted the moods of my children who are now talking back to me as rude as I was to them.

Fully aware that the alarms were starting to go off in my head urgently prompting a mood shift or else the shit was about to hit the fan. Watching in hopes of a sign to influence some sort of reset for the sake of us all. As I take a moment to myself to figure out exactly what is happening in this very moment, I am reminded that I too created a tool years ago for a way to help my son re-open his mind.

We had been sitting around the kitchen table one evening trying to help my son navigate his homework. It was obvious at the time that his frustration was getting the better of him as he just kept repeating that he did not understand how to get the answer. I had exhausted all of my old-school ways of explaining grade four math which got us nowhere, so I then resorted to pulling out a box of cookies from the cupboard.

However, before I had a chance to open the box and explain my mathematical method of dividing cookies, he burst into tears proceeding to insist that he needed to leave the table.

I remember feeling as if I could literally hear his mind slam shut as it refused to allow anyone in to help. We then proceeded to sit at the table for many moments as he whaled going on about how he hated homework and how mean we were for making him suffer through it.

Being a visual learner myself I realised in that moment that if I explained what feeling I had just experienced it may shed some light on his situation. Commencing to explain that when faced with difficult situations sometimes our mind likes to slam shut as I gesture striking my hands together in front of my face, palms over my closed eyes, 'just like a ninja karate chop', I exclaimed. This gesture instantly brought him back into the present moment and out of his negative cycling mindset.

I sat there for a few seconds eyes covered as I knew I now had his full attention after all, what child does not like to talk about ninjas? I can sense the calmness settle into his breathing as he too mimics my hand gesture making his own chop sound as he begins to relax. I continue to explain that this is exactly what your mind is doing when faced with learning anything difficult, sometimes it just slams the door in frustration not wanting to see a solution.

As we both sit in this darkness now giggling, I ask him to see through his hands which are blocking out all signs of light. 'I can't mama', he replies, causing a few more giggles between the two of us. I then proceed to invite him to take in a deep breath. With that breath reminding him that as he releases his breath and opens his hands so will his mind be open. A mind open to a solution for him to see.

Using his breath as the key to open this door and as he removes his hands, we find ourselves sitting there staring into each other's eyes. It was obvious that this tool made an impact on his very being as he jumped up to thank me with a massive loving hug. Sitting back down he then insisted that I share my math cookie secrets with him as he cracks open the cookie box with his mind wide open.

With this memory, it has created enough space for me to address my own mind slamming shut here today. The frustration of today's task list has triggered my mind to slam shut. I realised that this 'key reset' was again one of those vital tools which had the ability to change my life. However, never for myself as I perceive it as being as too juvenile to help an adult-size problem, never to implement it into my daily practice.

Why the hell not, I found myself stating aloud raising my hands up. I too want to be a ninja. As I ninja karate chop my hands quietly making that sound, I place my palms over my eyes blocking out the light and pausing for a moment in the darkness as I take a few cleansing breaths.

I proceed to tell myself that then when I open my eyes and remove my hands my mind too will be open. I could feel my spirit let out a slight giggle of pleasure as I had finally come full circle and implementing this 'key reset' into my own day. A day that minutes ago seemed so stressful and overwhelming were now being relieved with a simple technique, breath, an open mind, and a sense of fun.

Giving myself this 'key reset' to reopen my mind gifted me a direct connection with my spirit this morning.

10,000

As this journey progresses dealing with the stress of work seems to be a skill all on its own. I begin noting my incessant need to please others especially when getting caught up in the chaos of problematic situations. They say that to master any skill in life you need to have worked at it ten thousand times.

Seriously? This statement initially gave me mixed emotions depending on how I looked at it. On one hand, ten thousand times seems to be an unachievable repetition for anything and anyone because frankly who has the time to do anything, ten thousand times?

Yet, on the other hand, ten thousand times if looked at as the number of chances one would get to attempt to master any given skill this outlook seems much more unconditional and attainable.

This viewpoint brought hope that I too could work towards attaining my true potential at any given task I was willing to focus on. It released the undo stress I was currently experiencing. Similar to having an unlimited supply of chances to screw it up if necessary and time to figure out the best way to learn from each failure on the road to achieving it.

This art of mastering skills is well documented and is duly noted that it will take time and patience for one to become proficient in any given skill. Much like the earliest of skills that we have mastered like walking or talking.

However, I realise it is my conditioning around the mindset of mastering a task, a pressing issue needed to be addressed. Embracing this new concept that we literally can get 'ten thousand chances' has opened my mind and my heart to my true potential and revealed the people pleaser in me. The pleaser seemed to be intertwined with trying to match others' behaviours in hopes of pleasing them. While the importance put on them outweighed my own experience.

Acknowledging that work much like daily life has the ability to bring out the worst or the best in a person as it slowly morphed us into something we may or may no longer align with. In this people-pleaser state, I was no longer aligned with my purpose of creating a positive impact in my life. This people-pleaser was more focused on proving my own self-worth to others.

Once again noticing even at work I was putting more value on what others thought of me than on how I valued myself. This state often paralyzes me with fear of ever wanting more. More respect. More patience. More understanding. More support.

This 'key reset' shifted this people-pleaser exposing it once and for all. I felt a sense of letting go of restrictions and the value I had placed on other people's expectations. Acknowledging that the only person you can ever truly please, or fix is yourself. Which I now graciously accept each of these 'ten thousand chances' which I may need to master self-worth.

Reality check-in: Day 155

Mind check-in:

Work has been stressful; however, I still feel like a ninja rocking the key reset.

Body check-in:

Started walking again.

Spirit check-in:

Now that I have a more consistent taste for connection, I want more.

Today I am looking forward to my visit with a close buddy, Anne. Even if it is a quick social distance visit. As we hang out at the end of the driveway, she informs me that the Covid saga continues with an increase in cases and a rising death toll. As a nurse who works at our local hospital, she updates me with a few covid stats then quickly informs me that she now will be moving into a camper at the end of her mom's property. I had heard of the current strain being felt by our front-line workers but did not fully understand the scope of this impact until now.

I could only imagine the stress and strain of returning home after a long shift wondering if one was arriving home with more than their tired feet but with Covid.

As I listened to her new plan of setting up a safe living arrangement, I could not help but feel overwhelmed by the thought of separation that she would be going through. Missing out on nightly cuddles, conversations and not to mention all the hugs and kisses as an overwhelming feeling of fear and separation would increase each day.

As we ended our conversation, I head back into the house finding myself scouring the internet for worldwide covid stats before I could realise what I was doing. Quickly I remind myself to limit it to one minute. Get the facts and get out resulting in me finding out that 95,000 people worldwide have died of Covid which left me with little hope that tomorrow will be better.

The stress of Covid once again seems to be flooding through my body as I set down my phone mad that I had let it weasel its way back into our home. I decide to head for a cold shower to try to wash away this fear and bring me back to the present moment. As I stood there letting the icy water run down my body it shocks my mind back to the present moment.

A present moment that I am at home, safe, healthy, alive, being able to feed my children and pay my bills. This brings my awareness even more present as I sense the water running down my body, how good the water feels and just how strong my body feels standing still.

Instantly this makes me feel connected to nature and the waters' ability to wash away some of the stress and tension. I take in a deep cleansing breath to release the building stress even more. This allows the space in my mind to feel the calm and clear thoughts as I remind myself of my simple Covid plan.

A simple covid plan of what is actually happening to you right here and right now. Is there anything that you can do to positively influence this present situation? Feel the emotions that come, cry if needed, reset my mindset, breath and repeat.

Looking back on my past has made me realise that I do have the ability to deal with and overcome a lot. The key now would be not to stuff it all in down deep instead allowing myself to feel with each emotion for what it was. Acknowledging and feeling the emotion for what it was without judgement of right or wrong allowing the awareness that the emotion was present. Creating space which would then make room to deal with these feelings without judgement. Right here and now as the last thing I wanted to do with this whole Covid situation was just to stuff it all down just to have to deal with a stress-related disease later in life.

As my husband Kevin arrived home that night, I gave him the update about my girlfriend moving into a trailer for safety's sake. He could sense my stress levels begin to rise once again so with a smile he broke into the conversation asking me, 'when are we going to hammer out the details for our positive project'.

It was time to do something, anything creative that made us feel alive as life and our focus seemed to be guiding us back to the covid fog. One thing was for sure I knew that I needed something else to focus on, so my thoughts instantly went back to the inspiring brainstorming session I had a few weeks prior.

A plan would need to be implemented so after much discussion of what we enjoyed, we agreed a decision needed to be made and to just pick something. Anything. Stop waiting for the perfect idea, or perfect plan. Stop saying we should do something positive, and just do something positive. Keeping it simple and focusing on inspirational things we loved such as our love of music, nature, positive influence, and the simple fact that we were tech-savvy.

Our imperfectly perfect idea was sparked and funny enough we decided to start up a YouTube meditation music channel. Our mission statement was a simple one, do something positive that makes a positive ripple of energy for ourselves and others. Excited now at the prospect that we could do this together keeping our minds active with positive influence. We then set our goal to create one hundred positive videos with no specific timeline. Yes, there would be challenges of learning something new, of spending most of our free time creating this positive ripple but for once in a long time we felt inspired and hungry for more. After all, we had ten thousand chances to figure out how to create positive change through these videos.

"Pain is certain. Suffering is optional." — Unknown.

Fuck... My dear friend Anne just texted me to say that she has tested positive for Covid and is now feeling extremely sick.

I had been wondering what they were up to. Noticing that we had missed our usual text messages to check in on each other. As I allowed my initials feelings of worry, fear, and frustration to surface I began to fully embrace the uncomfortable emotions that they brought.

Tears began to stream down my face as I sat for a moment allowing these emotions their rightful place before I text her back. Acknowledging the fear, anger, and sorrow that this text brought I became very still.

Breathe.

Bringing my thoughts from fear to gratitude as I allowed my breath to calm me and create some space. Instead of it sending me into my usual pity party, it sent me into a mission of how I can help. Help with a mix of overwhelming gratitude for my own family's health and the health of the rest of her family. Thankfully, she was the only one in her family who tested positive.

Not only did Covid give me a reality check it also seemed to bend time as it messed up with our usual way of life. Leaving us with much-needed reflection time whether we wanted it or not.

A gift to surrender to the new way of life of choices to take chances to better oneself.

As fighting this new way of life and yearning for the old way only left me feeling miserable and unsatisfied. This Covid reality check was forcing me to sit face-to-face with myself. As I looked in this giant mirror reflecting all that I am. My very existence, accomplishments, and failures. Overshadowing these failures and accomplishments with overwhelming gratitude for life and the ability to choose to create something amazing with this life I was given.

CHAPTER 10

Five A.M. reality call. Get the fuck up!

Snooze, snooze again, excuses rush in, snooze again, roll over, more excuses, snooze again as I sense sadness tightening its grip. Snooze again realising this time that there is no way I will still be on time if I do not get up right this minute. Jumping out of bed I proceed to rush around like a chicken with its head cut off following my typical morning routine of frantic energy leaving no doubt in my mind that this process was contributing to the strength of sadness's grip.

Getting up has shed light on this reoccurring sadness, feelings of disappointment and even boredom with the state of my life. I realised that I did not have any issues popping out of bed on a day that I was looking forward to or committed to show up for.

However, most of my days I laid in bed wanting and feeling a deep desire for just one more snooze. Justifying to myself that I was happy and motivated to start my day once my feet hit the floor. That I was a doer, who loved to hustle and get shit done once I managed to get up. Seriously what did I need to get up for.

My kids were now older and so sufficient at getting themselves up, dressed and fed that they did not need me anymore. I loved my bed and sleeping going so far as to say to myself that I had to sleep in because my body required more sleep. Or just one more snooze, because I did not sleep well that night even though I had already had eight hours of sleep confirming that I was definitely not part of any five-a.m. club.

Intermittently I have been using a method to get up over the past few months with little to no success. Probably due to the fact that this was one of those many tools that I had heard about, and thought was so great but never actually used. Never implemented it into each day to reap all the benefits it had to offer instead exhausted by giving into the many excuses.

Once accepting that this was one of those great methods that I heard about but did not implement. Reminding myself that the keyword is 'heard' as heard is only hearing about a method, and 'learned' is learning to actually put it into practice. Gone are the days of feverishly consuming all and any self-growth information I could find as today would be a day of implementing.

Knowing that all the progress this year was due to the fact that I was willing to slow down and learn to use tools that the universe had nudged me towards. The real magic started to happen as I taped into a method that would help me get the fuck up ridding myself of my addiction to snoozes. One gloriously simple counting method that would change the way I viewed and started my day. It goes something like this when my alarm goes off, I count down five, four, three, two, one and then get up out of bed, quickly.

When I say quick, I mean quick, before all my excuses have a chance to rush in, excuses that loved to taunt me with the warmth and comfort of my bed. This simple five-four-three-two-one method was something I picked up from Mel Robbins an amazing author and social media maven. Her practical life hack helped break years of habitual snooze conditioning. Not only has this method helped get me out of bed but it opened my eyes up to the inspiration of the day. No more snoozes, no more mind games, no more excuses just one little hack to break the cycle of years of conditioning. Allowing me to get up before my shitty attitude had a chance to wake up.

Acknowledging that I seem to be at my weakest and my shitty attitude was at her strongest while I hit that snooze button numerous times. Snooze for me was like a drug, a drug that gave me instant relief but never really made me feel any better, ultimately resulting in feeling worse. Worse as it filled me with feelings of guilt and sadness for not having control over getting up.

However, the bright side of acknowledging this guilt is that it brought to light the need to find out why I really did not want to get up. Knowing that there was no such thing as just one snooze for me anymore. In order to break this conditioning, I needed to just do it. I needed to get up out of bed without a single snooze.

This very thought made me feel as if I was losing out on something or having to give up my favourite food which is why I associate it with being addicted to repetitively pressing the snooze. I would need to rip that Band-Aid off and get up without a single snooze as I rehabbed myself. The agreement I made with myself was that once that alarm went off the first time, count down and get the fuck up. Do not think just quickly get up and for heaven's sake, get up before all the excuses come rushing in because they would and will, every single time.

"The early bird gets the worm." — John Ray

Yes, the early bird does get the worm, but I wanted to sleep in and have breakfast in bed with warm bagels, avocados, and eggs, not worms. What person in their right mind would get up for worms? Apparently, me! Eventually, I would get up and start to enjoy that juicy worm each day so never say never if you too happen to be that night owl disagreeing with a five-a.m. start. If I can get up at five a.m. anyone can.

However, if you thought I just decided to wake up one day and count down my little five, four, three, two, one and miraculously popped out of bed after a few weeks of using this method and instantly become a morning person that would be the farthest thing from the truth. For me this has been a slow crawl inching my way from eight a.m. closer to five a.m. with a few less snoozes-accepting that slow is better than not at all, because at least I am still moving forward.

"You are not tired. You are uninspired." — Unknown

I really suck at becoming a morning person and finally admit to myself that my current morning routine was blocking this healing process realising that to date I had exactly one hundred and fifty days left to heal myself. Apparently to release the sadness and find my true motivation for waking up each day and not the false motivation of measured accomplishments and completed tasks. No longer wanting to get up for the sake of pleasing others I torturously began releasing the precious value that I had given these mundane tasks which seemed to have drained the life from me.

I had come a long way but still had a lot to address. Between work, and being a mom and wife, I seemed to have lost sight of myself. Sight of what made me happy as I had been so busy trying to keep everyone else around me happy that I lost myself, especially my self-worth. I knew my snooze addiction was somehow rooted in this need to please others. Realising that maybe, just possibly, I was procrastinating getting up to the thought of pleasing others. Snoozing away my life granting to give myself just a little more time.

Grief seems to be the response to loss, particularly to the loss of someone or some living thing that has died, to which a bond or affection was formed. As I delved deeper and deeper into why I felt such a need to be a pleaser I realise that my morning routine was tied up in grief. A deep grief which was the reaction to my loss, particularly in the loss of myself. I needed to prioritize making time for myself. The time that would allow me a greater connection to my soul understanding that when I truly felt connected and grateful other people's negative energy did not affect me.

Knowing this connection was now possible if only I could address that my life had little to no balance left sensing a pull to slow down and enjoy the process of challenging myself. Challenging myself to slow down to pursue the commitment to work through and grow each day. I was on a mission to find a meditation, mentor or something that could help create a safe space. A safe space to reconnect. As I scrolled through my phone this evening, I asked the universe to point me in the right direction for a meditation to help me find myself.

The first thing that I saw when I opened my phone was a three-day online meditation class. One benefit that this damn Covid situation had brought was that social media was now flooded with positive influencers. Influencers which typically were once only at live events at some far-off destination. Covid now allowed me to attend right here in my home so as I looked into a few different meditation weekends I kept feeling a strong pull. A pull back to the first post that had popped up on my phone. Maybe it was the price, maybe it was the fact that it started in four days or just how familiar I was with the presenter.

'That's it, I am doing it,' I chirped aloud. Not sure how I am going to take all this time for myself, but I am doing it. Three whole days spent on self-meditation and growth.

Day one.

Day one of my three-day meditation course ended up just being a bully sales workshop woven into some meditation and motivational talks. Very disappointing, however, in these situations I turn to the universe with questions. Why did I sign up for this course? Why am I going through this particular situation? Or what is it that I am supposed to be seeing and learning from all of this? Why did I feel such a pull to sign up for this course if it was crap?

As I feel the disappointment and sadness take hold, my mind slams shut. I stop, breathe and key reset my mind hoping to no longer be focused on what was wrong with this class but attempting to open my mind and eyes up to the positive potential. As I sit there with the palms of my hands over my eyes focusing on my breathing and opening my mind, I allow all the feelings of being upset and wasting my weekend on something that was clearly not what they promised to begin to melt away. I opened my eyes continuing my intentions on carrying myself to something more positive. As the day continued, I begin to feel all the positive energy that everyone on the call brought. Even right down to the stretches that they had us do throughout the day and how grateful my body felt to be moving.

Day two.

I got up at five a.m. again to attend my meditation course. Fighting to keep my mind open even through the presenter's condescending comments that the universe only gave limited chances to you totally pissed me off. The universe is unconditional, and we choose to come to be here to learn. Seriously, if we had a limited number of chances, we would all be fucked. This was simply just a sales tactic. A sales tactic which I would need an open mind to be able to see through in order to see anything positive with this experience even if it meant I did not agree with his methods.

As I lay in bed tonight, mulling over my day. That is when it happened. I got it. I finally understood what the big reason was that the universe had led me here, to this very moment. The most pivotal part of this class would be the start time. A start time of eight a.m. which translated to five a.m. my time. Once realising the time change after I signed up, I really did not think twice about getting up. Equating it to the fact at the time that it was because I was excited to do this meditation course. Even after realising shortly into day one, I was no longer excited for the course.

So, *why* did I not have an issue with getting up on day two for this meditation course?

After all, this was a course that I was not even enjoying. The answer was simple because I felt obligated to. Once again filling a need to please someone else, but why? The fee was so minimal.

Seriously, why could I get out of bed with little to no drama for something I was not excited for instead only getting up over feeling obligated to attend *but I could not get up for myself.*

My true level of self-worth came crashing down. What the fuck, I said to myself. I know in my heart that *I am so worth getting up for*. I felt shivers go up my spine and went to sleep knowing something had definitely shifted.

Day three.

That third morning of class was the first day in my life that I would get up truly and fully just for me. Not because of work, and not because I had signed up for a meditation class. Not even for my husband and kids, or because we were doing anything exciting such as travelling to the airport to catch an early flight but for *me*, just me. Thank you, self for once again realising in that moment that getting up at five a.m. was one more way of saying that I did care for myself. That I did see and value my own worth and that I did in fact want to give myself more.

Reality check-in: Day 223.

Mind check-in:

No snooze. Got up. No drama.

Body check-in:

Body is feeling so happy and strong from the amazing walk this morning.

Spirit check-in:

Taped in and turned on.

I did it, yah me, I have arrived.

It only took seven months of slowly inching my way to the five-a.m. marker to get up, five million snoozes later. Years of conditioning have finally been broken; I have officially become part of the five-a.m. club. A club I had heard numerous times about. A crazy concept of getting up at five a.m. to kick-start your day. It was a method of taking charge and making time for myself. I now get up just for me, no one else, not my kids, not my job, but for me. It has taken me days of getting up at five a.m. to even admit that I was now doing it and that it was a new habit probably because I was afraid of slipping back into my addiction to a multi-snooze life.

Getting up early not only started to create more time it started to create a deeper drive to reflect on myself. In the beginning what seemed to be harshly judging my own behaviour became a game of little fixes resulting in a much more fulfilled day not to mention, time to drink a cup of coffee relaxing just like it was Saturday morning, every morning. I now had time to even take a walk, swim or even a little meditation and yoga if I so desired allowing time with and for myself to set the tone for my day.

When I had first heard of the five a.m. club, I was almost disgusted. Who and how could anyone willingly get up at five a.m. if they had the choice to sleep in longer? How and why would this be of any benefit to anyone? Especially me and definitely not possible as I require more sleep than the average person. Now reflecting back all these excuses just sounded hilarious realising just how lame they really were. How my shitty attitude loved the sadness and hated personal growth knowing its very existence relied on those snoozes.

Thanks to the simple but powerful counting method I find that I have the same amount of energy whether I got seven or nine plus hours of sleep but with way less drama and fight to get up. As I evaluated who and what I was getting up for made all the difference. You may be thinking but how can counting down get me out of bed because this is a short quick and easy habit which does not take any effort other than your speed. Speed to get up before your mind does.

Laughing now as it seemed to almost shock me that it did indeed work at breaking the cycle of my conditioning and mindset that I was not a morning person. Squashing the idea that getting up at five a.m. was just for workaholics and people who could not slow down enough and enjoy life. Realising it was the complete opposite as it gave me a choice to choose myself. A choice to start my day with positive energy and a strong belief in my own self-worth as I gave myself time before I gave it to anyone else.

This five-a.m. club also brought forward simple awareness that would allow me to get an instant sense of where my mind was at for the day. Right when I woke up was my mind filled with gratitude or was yesterday's drama over a minor mistake made? Bringing my awareness without judgement that I was once again caring more about what someone else thought of me, than what I thought of myself.

As my self-worth starts to take over the people pleaser, a rush of pride washes over me. Pride of just how much growth had developed, inspiring a solid ability to help carry me through my day. Caring less and less about what others thought of me as I made each choice reminding myself to focus on what felt good to me. Quickly realising that this simple tool could also be used for many other things than just getting up in the morning such as getting my ass off my phone, dealing with anxiety and stress. Even sharing this method with my kids to help them to create space between their thoughts and their reactions.

Reality check-in: Day 232

Mind check-in:

On a roll, feeling as if my mind was finally starting to be a team player.

Body check-in:

Created my own five a.m. club for myself. Feeling pretty proud. Stronger each day.

Spirit check-in:

Feeling more empowered that I recognize the pleaser and slowly replacing it with self-worth. Happy Birthday to me.

As I lay in bed tonight reflecting on how much I enjoyed my birthday celebrations I am taken aback by emotion. Never being a big fan of my own birthdays due to past baggage these yearly birthday occurrences seemed to have weighed me down.

Tonight, however, I felt overwhelming gratitude, for my health, my personal growth, and my willingness to look within. An acceptance that brought me to this very moment after forty-seven years I could and would celebrate me, for being me. The good, the bad and even my shitty attitude. Understanding that this was going to be a pivotal year. However, celebrating myself on my birthday was not one of my wildest dreams as I reflected back on what a great time I had today.

All the laughs, food, and quality time I spent together with my husband and kids. As my kids approach their pre-teens, I realise just how quickly time goes by and try to embrace each phase of their own growth as it comes.

Admitting that I had been finding it hard to connect with both my kids from time to time as they naturally evolved out of the Mommy, I love you phase to the Mom, you already told me that phase. Making days like today worth being in the moment to really take in and enjoy their ever-evolving personalities aware that these amazing memories had the power to impact them as well.

"Children are the living messages we send to a time we will not see". — John F. Kennedy.

There seems to be a fine line between working on oneself and being consumed by the ego of oneself. A delicate balance of receiving and not taking as getting up at five a.m. has given me plenty of time for self-growth it has also made me very territorial over this cherished time.

Over the past few days my son overheard me expressing my gratitude and excitement for my newfound start time so, around six a.m. every morning he emerged with the same eager excitement to start his day and have some one-on-one time with us. The first morning I was delighted to see his happy little face however, after the thirty-minute conversation that followed it left me feeling much less satisfied as my self-imposed journaling schedule was being cut into.

A routine of delving within and documenting this journey had taken over so hard that even my son's presence in the room seemed less important than my task at hand. Now my ego had joined forces with my shitty attitude threatening as they reared their ugly heads filled with self-imposed limitations, creating my very own roadblock. Justifying my negative thoughts about having only had a few hours each morning for self-reflection before I started my full-time job.

By the fifth morning in a pissed-off voice I say to my husband, 'I got up early to work on myself and have done little to nothing because Spencer is interrupting my flow.' It is at that very moment I become fully aware of the now abrupt negative downward spiral of my energy, as I hear Spencer creak his way up the stairs sure that he has heard me. No apologies here and almost too embarrassed to record these words acknowledging my adult-size tantrum of being consumed in my own self-pity and anger. As the rude questions and comment bombard the air and squash any site of positive energy the comment under my breath starts to take form.

Why does no one understand? Kevin, you are not helping by visiting with him for thirty minutes before you leave for work. This does leave me with feelings of guilt mixed in with anger but still not enough to shift and make a choice even though Spencer has now retreated to his room. As Kevin leaves for work he bends to give me a quick kiss and says, "I love you." But I can tell by his tone he is not impressed. Kevin then reminds me I still have over an hour left to dig into my process. I hiss that it is going to take me that long just to get back into it as I am left wallowing in my own self-pity staring at my keyboard. Claiming my parent of the year award.

As the anger subsides and the guilt emerges, I pause and reflect on my words, thoughts and actions that just ensued like verbal diarrhoea never to consider any ways to make it stop. I know in this moment I just need to breathe and acknowledge that my shitty attitude is trying its best to take over. Knowing full well that a reset is in order, I plug my headphones into my phone hoping to reset myself with something inspiring to listen to.

Music is another go-to reset for me as I whole heartedly believe that music heals the soul. I take a deep breath in and ask for some patience and guidance as I bring my attention back to this very moment. Opening my YouTube app, the first thing that pops up is a Mei-Ian seventeen-minute meditation for raising your vibration and streaming source energy into your life. Thankful for the sign as I know this was exactly what I needed in this very moment. Pressing play I sit there with my eyes closed breathing my way through, allowing her angelic voice to weave its way into my heart with each tone recentring me. I acknowledge that I have been struggling with the emotions that documenting this journey has stirred up and that my anger towards Spencer was just an excuse for my own natural decline in willingness to go deeper.

My eyes begin to well as I connect to how I must have made him feel as I squashed his positive energy this morning. I then begin to open myself up to her beautiful healing tones the music begins to heal and guide me. Understanding that we are all humans who do shitty things and sometimes act like a bitch but the key in all of this messiness is that am I evolving and learning from these mistakes.

Relaxing my mind as the music releases the guilt with each note hearing the universe calling to comfort me with unconditional love. Reminding me to be open and embrace life as it came but most importantly to release the importance, I put on daily tasks instead of embracing the relationships and people around me. I feel the stale parts of me breaking and falling away letting in a little light with each breath. The light that has the ability to crumble the wall that I had so meticulously created around my heart as I feel the connection once again. "You got this", my spark hummed along with the meditation.

As the meditation ends, I realise in this holy shit moment that true inspiration does come from friction. I begin making my rounds of apologies for this morning's bitchy behaviour, especially to the child who was excited to start his day with so much love for us. Knowing that I have much to learn from his enthusiasm for starting his day with constant heartfelt greetings and warm hugs.

Therefore, thank you, Spencer, thank you universe and thank you self for realising that my son's path once again is crossing mine in divine time. Thanking myself for not letting the cloud of anger and guilt of past conditioning block this teaching point as these are the very experiences of life which I draw inspiration from knowing it is never a clear or clean path.

CHAPTER 11

You are never too old for a good fart joke

Why is love like a fart? If you have to force it, it is probably crap.

The word "fart, shit and damn" all came up on Microsoft word as offensive. Which I thought was hilarious probably because I grew up in Saskatchewan. Or maybe just the simple fact that in today's society, we have become so restricted and sensitive to everything needing to be politically correct. A serious need for perfection with everything and everyone needing to be perfect, or something must be wrong with you.

Even poor Mr Potato Head cannot even be called Mr Potato Head any more. Seriously if we look closely enough at anything, we will always find fault with it and always find offence to be taken.

Feeding the ego with the need to point out and judge others as we are conditioned to be on high alert for anything that does not align with our current belief system. Relentlessly applying excessive pressure to always say the perfect thing, act the perfect way, or give the perfect answer.

How can anyone ever feel as if they are ever doing anything right? If everything we say or do is somehow upsetting someone, somewhere as we take every thought, word, or action so literally. I am all for equality and human rights but who will stand up for poor, Mr Potato Head? A guy who just wants to be that fun-loving toy that brought so much joy and hours of unrestricted play and fun to so many children. Children who did not have a care in the world nor created any preconceived ideas that Mr Potato Head was anything but pure fun, love, and joy.

Perfection is a state of completeness, flawlessness, or supreme excellence. Even the term perfection is used to designate a kindred concept which draws people into thinking this is the most desired state of being. Constantly bombarded in our society with images and expectations to look the perfect way, live in the perfect house, having the perfect job and be in the perfect relationship. For many years perfection used to be my endgame as I constantly strived for this completeness and flawlessness of excellence. Almost as if nothing else mattered unless it resulted in perfection. Acknowledging that instead of satisfaction it brought about pressure, guilt, and a deep sense of sadness as my focus on perfection needed to be achieved at all costs.

Until I decided to take this journey to heal myself and Covid hit that is. Covid has been one of the greatest gifts of clarity for me. Granting foresight that my need for perfection did not have the ability to bring about any true completeness or lasting satisfaction. The clarity that life is far from perfect and as I started to evaluate what was the importance that imperfection brought was actually invaluable to each day. Highlighting that it was not a clean house or the idea of a perfect relationship nor being perfect at my job that mattered but more so the journey of getting there as it began to shift my values. Seeing perfection for what it was a negative constant state of striving for completion. Often loses sight of life's true purpose of continual learning, growth, love, and giving unconditionally.

A shift in mindset was needed as perfection could no longer be my end goal but more of a state of being really, really, really, good at something as I attempt to enjoy the journey of the process. Working toward removing my focus solely on the outcome. Shitty situations much like Covid has given me clarity in this moment to stop and be grateful for where I am in this process. Taking note in that moment, no matter how hard I try; life will never ever be perfect. However, within this very imperfect moment of time, I find myself digging in to enjoy the true experience of this life.

As I sift through all the shit, I hold around perfection, I realise the illusion it presents. An illusion that perceived perfection as a sense of completeness and accomplishment. Ultimately creating a better person. Somehow, however, my ego had perceived this as creating a higher or better person. As if perfection had somehow given a person more human value. Ideally becoming a student of life with grace and awareness of the process that happens to achieve a goal. Even through a shitty attitude as I begin to understand that there is a serious need to let go of the ego in order to continually grow.

5

"Pick five".

In digging into my past, I continued to tap into previous tools as I added Jay Shetty's Think Like a Monk along my way. I had heard of a simple way to provoke growth within by checking to see what energy and emotions you were holding around different aspects in life. I instantly fell in love with the simplicity and speed of what I call the 'pick five' tool as it forced me to find answers. Not recalling the actual name of this tool and having adapted it into my own version that worked for me. I began rapidly connecting to the source of my people pleaser and why she lusted over perfection so intensely.

This is what you will need: a blank piece of paper, a pen, and an open mind.

Step One:

Ask yourself; What does blank mean to me? For me today I am digging into "Perfection".

Step Two:

Write down everything that comes to you as it may be thoughts, feelings, names of people, or events. (Aim for at least five emotions or events to surface. Do not judge just allow).

Done! This may take one minute or one hour, so I take whatever time I need to dig in. As the more I repeated this exercise the quicker I could identify the source or blockage.

Striving to dig into at least five emotions or events was not always apparent and more than not produced shocking answers that took time to accept. As accepting all those negative thoughts meant that these negative thoughts were mine. Often thoughts that came from deep within. Exhausting and painful with overwhelming emotions of just wanting to flee from the memory. In the beginning, this exhaustion was reinforced by my shitty attitude. She spouted on that, working through past emotions needed to be slow and painful if one wanted to even deal with them in the first place.

Or did it, as one morning while delving into the whole mess of perfection I started to wonder if the very concept of working through one's shitty baggage needed to be slow and painful or if it could be quick and painless. So as the shock of each negative mindset wore off, I began to see it as more of a game. A game that my playful competitive side loved to blast through as I raced my way into past negative emotions. Keeping it simple to the one word that I wanted to focus on like perfection, relationships, money, love, and power.

This effectively thought-provoking tool came with insight that was glaringly apparent. As I could identify one common thread woven throughout all the different conditioning of my shitty attitude, fear, and lack of self-worth. A common thread linking them together creating one strong force tying me to negative energy. Each thread noticeably traces right back to my childhood. A childhood that even the word perfection brings back memories of the need to keep the peace and make sure everything was perfect. As it echoed my need to please everyone else producing fear and resentment resulting in my shitty attitude.

"So much of the healing of our world begins in healing the inner child who rarely, if ever, got to come out and play". — Unknown.

As I peel back the many layers of perfection, I am quickly realising the complex conditioning it possesses. Many difficult emotions have surfaced some of which I had no idea were related to perfection but quickly realise that everything seems to be interrelated. By the third morning addressing triggers with five words, I could now sense that I was very close. Close to finding the root cause, reassuring myself that if I still feel this nagging drive to go deeper into perfection than relief will be found.

Pinpointing this crucial moment where perfections root emotion had imprinted its initial mark on my belief system.

Closing my eyes after gazing at the word "perfection" written on my paper, I recall all the emotions of not being enough floods over me with each emotionally charged wave. Sending a heaviness straight to my heart as the stress and strain of these emotions burst out of my chest in dire need of freeing themselves.

Never guessing as I wrote the word "perfection" on this paper the sheer magnitude of emotions. Deep emotions would surface causing a steady stream of tears to run down my cheeks dipping onto my page as it blurred the letters. I began feverously writing as one emotionally charged thought came after another. Wondering if I was even going to be able to understand my illegible handwriting from the sheer speed at which it was unloading from me. Much like the feeling you get when you have eaten too much spicey rich food and make a run for the bathroom unsure if you will make it. With the burning need to relieve yourself.

This urgent purge of charged emotion came to me as events and emotions all muddled together in the form of not feeling smart enough, good enough and valued enough as I carved it into the paper. Perfection seemed more like imperfection as I let it all flow. Memories of being alone, struggling in school, and an overwhelming sense of never being enough became compounded by the flood of anger, resentment and of course sadness. As I sat there staring at my now full piece of paper riddled with pen marks one final vivid memory broke through.

As vivid as I find myself sitting here writing at the table attempting to record this memory. A memory that I had not thought about for years. I could see myself as a child standing petrified in the middle of my bedroom as the sheer panic of hearing my dad's screaming voice quickly approaching my bedroom. He stomps in heading straight for my dresser adding at the top of his lungs what a pigsty the state of my room was in. I look around not sure what he is talking about as everything looks to be in its place.

Opening each drawer one by one he then proceeds to throw each piece of folded clothing onto my floor. Super charged with anger he suddenly turns with a burning rage in his eyes causing me to almost choke from his sheer disdain. He bee lines it for my closet still screaming and now adding in how ungrateful I was.

He then proceeds to forcefully push me into the closet, I could feel his spit of rage bouncing off my face as I collided with the back of the closet. Grabbing me and pinning me against the closet wall, confident that this was going to be my last day. I remember letting go.

My mind began screaming, "go ahead". "Go ahead and just do it". Only by the reaction in his eyes, I could tell that these words I screamed back were not in my head but aloud. Both stunned by my words he suddenly releases me as I crumbled to the floor sobbing, he turned still mumbling under his breath how useless I was as he slams my bedroom door closed.

As a child at the time, I did not see this as me taking back my power I viewed it as why am I so stupid because this is only going to make things worse.

Resulting in me questioning myself as to if I was sure my clothes were properly folded as I gaze at the only items in my bedroom which were a bed, dresser, and desk. So how could I possibly make it any cleaner? Doubting flooded in as to how I could have folded each piece of clothing differently recalling all my feeling of needing to somehow remedy this situation.

Understanding now, however, that no matter what I did as that young child nothing could have made that situation perfect or somehow created a perfect outcome.

As I sit at the table with this memory and all the emotions that came with it, I realise that I am not feeling any anger towards my dad but sadness for him and myself as that small innocent child.

Waves of sadness for my dad, an alcoholic with an alcoholic father who I can only image what type of conditioning was imprinted on him at a young age. Sadness how his own conditioning helped sculpt him into the man he is today. And of course, sadness for that small child. A sense of sadness for my feelings of not being good enough or doing enough. Sadness was that part of me that had somehow broken me that day.

Understanding that such an event does actually fracture us.

Now giving those unfiltered emotions of this event space, it gives me the ability to retrieve that piece of me that got left behind. Not to mention an ability to forgive my dad for his conditioning. With this forgiveness, I feel the relief that this gift of forgiveness brings.

Gifting me a peace of mind instead of willingly carrying around the pain which I had exhaustively been torturing myself with. It also gifted me clarity regarding his way of dealing with stress and his choice to take his anger out on those closest to him. Even regarding the way, he saved the best parts of himself for perfect strangers, either way, it really does not matter. All that mattered is that I found my first impression of perfection as it imprinted on my very being.

"If you love life, do not waste time, for time is what life is made up of". — Bruce Lee

This quote seems to have feed my inner ninja on so many levels. Possibly because I can recall even my mother telling me to enjoy time as it seems to speed up at an unbelievable pace as you get older.

So, as I wake up this morning, I feel so grateful to have woken up. Literally and figuratively. Knowing that today was not a given and understanding that to connect with my spark on a more consistent basis I would need to stay awake. Now allowing myself numerous resets throughout the day if needed to ensure that I was on track and awake.

Awake and on track.

These very words seem to spark my present situation in a positive manner. I knew a choice would need to be made. A pivotal choice of what I would and would not be willing to spend my precious time on.

Was I going to get wrapped up in yelling at my kids to clean their rooms for the umpteenth time? Or am I just going to shut the door and hope that one day they will be inspired to clean it without being asked? Taking the time to examine what perfection meant to me and all the emotional events trapped around even the word perfection. I realised just how fucked up my conditioning was around this concept.

Perfection at its finest.

Delving into the incessant need as a child to produce a perfectly clean room. Cleaning a room that was already cleanly attempting to portray the image of a perfect child who always did what she was told. Understanding the foundation of what I believed perfection to be.

Even more so the emotion I attached to it. The emotion of guilt of not being perfect. The guilt of thinking I could have done more or been more.

Perfection was not only choking out the inner child in me, but I am sure it was choking out the inner child in my own children. Perfection affected the way we communicated right down to every adventure we took. I had the uncanny ability of telling them the perfect way to do everything. By everything I mean everything.

Brush your hair. Brush your teeth. Make your lunch. Make your bed. Do your homework. Call your friends. Even recalling these tasks, I can recall hearing them say, 'Mom I already know how to do that!'

Me wondering why they said it with such an attitude. Only to know and understand in this moment that ten-plus years of saying the same thing never allowed them to peel and eat that damn banana any way they pleased. Ultimately with the same result must have been super irritating if not driving them insane.

Creating two little beings with such high expectations of perfection would end today. Today I will attempt to loosen the reins. So instead of trying to fix all of my past conditioning, I decide to take a step back and just observe my own children. Afterall our children are a mirror of us, showing us the conditioning, we have so graciously bestowed on them. As I observe my own children, they seem to have taken the opposite approach to needing perfection.

Are they worried that the counters are not perfectly wiped off before they can play a board game? Nope. Only that they had fun playing the game. Are they worried that their rooms are not clean? Nope. Instead, existing comfortably in their mess. A mess that brought up many uncomfortable emotions only in me.

So off I went to place myself in the middle of a mess to see what emotions surfaced. As I stood in the middle of my daughter's disaster of a room I was shocked by an unexpected emotion. I felt fear. Overwhelming fear crept up my spine and sent tingles up my neck like I was expecting my dad to walk into her room at any moment.

As if I was back standing in the centre of my childhood bedroom. Taking in a deep breath I quickly close my eyes, 'I AM safe.' I hear myself say out loud. Loving how extinctual and rapid this support from within is starting to form. I am strangely happy that I acknowledged and feel the full emotion of this fear. Allowing it to wash over me.

It is funny in a dysfunctional way how uncomfortable a messy house made me feel. I get it!

I know understand what and why I get that icky feeling when my own house is messy. The sheer panic and need to clean and keep everything in its place. Resulting from years of conditioning which I continued to feed into as an adult. As I picked up that piece of me that I left behind that day as a child I feel such a sense of joy. An overwhelming joy and relief that I was not being left behind.

Reality check-in: Day 240
Mind check-in:
Searching for fun in my day is proving to be difficult.
Body check-in:
No snoozes no drama loving it.
Spirit check-in:
My connection feels so strong when I am having fun and enjoying the moment.

Letting go of perfection came to me in baby steps. It first started as the need to let go of my need to have a perfectly clean house twenty-four-seven. Yep, you heard it right no surprises here. Sure, I clean my house but the need for everything to have the perfect spot, all items to face a perfect way, be folded in a perfect manner and be cleaned in the perfect high standard of cleanliness needed to be let go. In some weird way, it has allowed me to feel more ok in difficult times.

OK and confident in knowing that I could get through any messy situation that life threw my way. As life is always going to get messy but that sometimes even within that messiness is fun, adventure and freedom all of which could be enjoyed.

As my need for perfection in my house became much more relaxed and a ten-second tidy became extremely rewarding. Releasing the need to spend countless hours begrudgingly cleaning and then begrudgingly pissed off after that it was not staying in that perfectly clean form. My house in a weird way started to feel cleaner than ever before even though it was not. I was now able to see where and who I would spend my time with. Instead of vacuuming my house for the second time this week became a bike ride with my daughter. Allowing my house to really feel lived in, creating a spark with signs of life that could now be felt.

Signs which said relax and enjoy life. To stop trying to predict and control every single outcome. Allowing my children in all their wisdom in their own individual ways continually had much to teach me. Reminding me when I ask them what they are planning on doing with their day. They usually just say I do not know. Is a good thing. Which use to totally piss me off, because if you did not have an exact plan of action of what you planned to do, that must have meant that you were planning on wasting your day. How could you have a successful day if you did not have a plan? I needed to continue working on releasing my need of even preplanning my own day. Instead, focus my intension to be in the present moment.

I knew I had a lot to learn from the art of playing and being in the moment. Being aware that my growth depended on me no longer letting perfection choke out the child in me. The child in me who loves adventure and running along the beach bare foot squealing with excitement. The child without a care in the world, only being in that moment. A child in me who I have found when given the space to really explore life could–fully experience joy and excitement. A child who could be in the moment and could magically return if needed any given time. Never worrying about perfection but just about feeling good and enjoying life at this very moment.

"Music acts like a magic key, to which the most tightly heart opens". — Maria Von Trapp

Melodies from the sound of music still twirling through my mind and heart after I read this quote. Music is similar to laughter which has the powerful ability to heal. While listening to a recent pod cast my friend Nikki had produced about using music to release stress seemed so simple. Yet, why do I not do it more? Or not at all. I can remember fond memories of singing and dancing away for no apparent reason other than because I wanted to.

It had been years since I danced away and enjoyed the music of life. Whether through singing in your car or dance parties in your kitchen. Allowing yourself to let loose and have fun. As an adult, I had forgotten how fun and how much I loved dancing. Getting totally lost in the song. Laughing at my seriously weird Seinfeld & Elaine dance moves. Not giving a crap what anyone else thinks as I laid it all out there. Music definitely had the power to heal. A healing process which I knew even thinking about dancing would allow my heart to open.

Knowing that an open heart allows all the good vibes to flow in. Currently, my days had been filled with work and self-growth both of which I enjoyed. For the majority of my day as with most jobs there were things that caused stress. Stress that could be relieved by taking a mental break with music. Music that could instantly bring me back into the moment and melt away the negative unwarranted urgency for perfection no matter who or what was pressing me. Music recreated a connection with the teenager in me who loved spending the day laughing, dancing, or singing. Cruising along Broadway Street rocking out to Madonna with my best friend in her red Fiero. Realising today that there was currently little to no fun in my day-to-day life. I needed to let the music in and heal me.

Reality check-in: Day 250
Mind check-in:
Searching for way to embrace the kid in me.
Body check-in:
A few too many bars of ice-cream this weekend.
Spirit check-in:
Excited for what is to come. Nervous but excited.

Today apparently, I am taking a break from the positive.

Augh! Some days Covid really pisses me off as we are currently in lock down *again*. Focus on the positive, nope, not today. The kids have been doing on-line schooling which means that as preteens they spend the full day on the screen only to wrap up their day with a quick snack and more screen time to chill out and game with their friends.

I am overwhelmed with a sense of failure as a parent. A neglectful parent when I see just how much time and how consumed by tech that they are becoming with each day that passes. Harping at them to get outside or that our self-imposed Tuesday and Thursday tech-free days are not being abided by. Leaving me feeling totally defeated as the negative side of effect of Covid seems to have sucked the fun right out of life. Hypnotizing them with videos of other kids playing and mishaps skateboarding if only I could offer something as exciting and fun to draw them out of their rooms.

It is not only their tech addiction that *Covid* has been amplified but feed my own addition to tech. Early morning documenting on tech which switches to working all day from home on tech morphing into a few videos at night and weekends on tech. As I claim my mother of the Year Award, I reassure myself that I am not alone as many have all lost touch with each other in a search to satisfy and soothe oneself during Covid gave me little to no comfort. I continue to ignore just how scary, dependent and life-sucking tech had become even in our home. Hoping for a shift tomorrow.

As I awake feeling positively inspired and determined to make today a positive one, I head upstairs for breakfast. I make my way to the kitchen and realise hours later into my day that no one has surfaced. Our kids who could play Lego, board games, or run around outside for hours, were now binge-watching Tik Tok and YouTube for hours on end. Only stopping to eat and pee. Seriously effecting their moods and attitudes. I needed to stop fighting about tech and worrying about everyone's mental health. I needed to try something new.

So, what does one do? I turn to tech. It is funny how reliant I too had become even if it was for positive growth. A video of Mel Robbins and her son pops up on my social feed. He had the best advice. Funny, a teen giving a forty-year-old parenting advice may seem an unlikely combination. But seriously he has been the best tool to tap into to.

He commented that as children our bad behaviours are learned from our parents. We are sponges! He comments. We mirror what we see as we grow up. Instead of saying "why are you sad" you could say, "hey I had an incredibly sad day today" and then share your feelings about your own day. Leading by example. Allowing your kids to know that sad feelings are normal and that expressing them is a healthy way to help break that bad habit. Acknowledging that their addiction to tech is a direct mirror of our parenting. Reminding me to stop daily at the end of our day and get outside no matter what the weather. Even if it is just for a drive to crank the music and decompress.

Reality check-in: Day 258

Mind check-in:

Observing obvious gaps in my parenting which is a good thing.

Body check-in:

Making better food choices over the last few days. Feeling its good effects.

Spirit check-in:

Feeling some major shifts and growth.

The expected value is also known as the expectation of the first moment. Never have expectations of parenting and decision-making seemed so imperative than it does right now. As the start of the school year approaches bringing with it gripping stress. The stress of deciding whether to send one's children to school or enrol them to online classes during a pandemic is overwhelming. Frankly neither of which seemed to be a great option.

As a parent the expectation to make critical decisions weighed heavily on my mind so as the first day of school made its way here, there were countless discussions on what to do. Online classes or send them to school. Both hosting extraordinarily strong pros and cons which neither seemed to be pointing at the right decision. Online school while it would keep them safe and healthy at home had serious repercussions on too much time spent on tech not to mention a lack of socializing with friends. On the other hand, sending them to school meant sending them into the germ farm with a serious risk of them getting Covid or passing Covid on to our ageing extended family.

At this point, I do not know definitively which would be the lesser of the two evils. As we flip-flopped back and forth between sending them to school and online schooling with the stress and fear of something happening to their little bodies.

"Parenting is the easiest thing in the world to have an option about, but the hardest thing in the world to do". — Matt Walsh

Staring down at my keyboard today I am very aware that doubt was starting to fester. Similar to a painful deep pimple which had been brewing for weeks. It started with a few delayed journaling sessions. A couple of sleep-ins followed by a few snoozes. Numbing myself with Netflix and scrolling social media. Finally admitting that the stress of Covid, especially of deciding on whether or not to send the kids to school had been festering. Festering into puss-filled feelings of doubt, procrastination, and guilt.

I sat back from my keyboard closed my eyes and took a cleansing breath. "What am I so afraid of?" I let the thoughts flood in. I found it usually took about five to ten thoughts of "what", to really get the juicy facts. Those juicy facts of what I was afraid of. Allowing myself to just sit with all these uncomfortable feelings and thoughts. Without judgement just observing. As these thoughts slowed right down, I sat with one lasting lingering thought.

That I am afraid of losing one of them. What if they got covid and died? I sat with this feeling. Trying to notice where in my body I felt it. I noticed a heaviness across my chest and tension in my neck and shoulders. As if my heart and shoulders were being squeezed in a vice, OK this was good. Allowing myself to be aware. Feeling the pressure and sheer physical weight it brought. Closing my eyes brought me back to this present moment. I took in a cleansing breath. Knowing that if I could just allow myself to fully feel and acknowledge that these feelings were there. Not to fix. Not to judge. Just to be aware that it existed. It would allow space to enter. Space that had the ability to release and relieve the heaviness in my shoulders and heart.

Finally, a decision would be made to send the kids to school. With a backup plan of course that if the shit hit the fan, we would pull them at Thanksgiving or sooner if needed. As they stand in front of our hedge for their inaugural first-day-of-school photo my heart sinks and I start to feel the tears well. This time allowing the pressure in my chest and shoulder to be felt and acknowledged. Before I know it, I am sitting in the car watching them walk into the school.

Filling me with guilt that I should have just kept them home safe and sound, but my husband Kevin reassures me that they need the structure. Not to mention the social aspect of seeing friends will be less stressful on them.

Even the word expectation can brew up stress. Expectation to make the perfect choices for my kids.

Expectation to be the perfect wife. Expectation to be the perfect employee. With all these expectations I began to wonder what my expectation for myself were. To date I had given little to no expectations for myself it was more about what others thought and needed. As I start to dial it back and be in the moment. Expectations start to turn to reflections of life and back on my goals of giving and making this lifetime one to enjoy and cherish.

As I worked away each day from home on the computer. I realise just how much I am missing human connection. The human connection I used to feel as I travelled with my job to work events as my need to give back to my community was no longer met. Covid has thrown a wrench in my current career. I know the universe is hinting to me that it is time for growth and change. Even making inspirational videos did not seem to fulfil this void of connection. As with all of my careers and different cities, I have lived in I have gone with the flow of where life takes me. But lately, this flow of life seems to be taking me down a path I did not find fulfilling. The friction of these feelings usually meant change is coming. Change that has the ability to help me grow and give back. I know these feelings of being stuck will not last. Realising that stuck is also a choice.

Work is work and home is home. Has always been my clear guideline and mindset. But as the stress of my day job has started to bleed into my home life. I had had enough. Working hard and getting tasks done no longer seems to be enough. A constant need to prove my worth had settled in. After realising that I was caring more about what other's expectations were instead of my own expectations. I really needed to just stop and observe without judgement.

What are my expectations *of myself?* But more importantly what are the expectations *for myself?*

Pleasing others had become my full-time job. When in reality what a person thinks of me is irrelevant. No matter how much importance I gave to their opinion of me. But my conditioning over releasing their power over me is the real mental battle. Currently what I thought of myself seems to only be the direct reflection of what I thought others thought of me. Constantly trying to please, to do a good job, to meet other's expectations. But now I see clearly that this is a choice. A choice to put more importance into what I knew to be true about myself.

CHAPTER 12

Guilty till proven innocent

As I delve into all the expectations, I have of myself and others, I seemed to have allowed guilt to be my primary lead instead of innocence and belief in others. A bitchy judge welding her gavel.

Guilty. Guilty. Guilty.

Right down to the smallest of issues. Who took my phone charger? Who left the dog outside? Who ate the last ice cream bar? Looking to blame in order to get to the bottom of whoever did these heinous crimes.

My emotions did not always make sense or warrant the crime. Somewhat shocking me each time I unleashed them. It did however bring my attention to the need to understand just how these bitchy oversized emotions worked. Understanding the basic concept and process of feelings that people experience. I had heard many spiritual and personal growth mavericks speak of raising your vibration and moving to a higher emotion. But seriously what did all of this mean?

My basic concept of emotions had been based off of whether I was happy or sad. Viewing anger or joy as the extent of how I currently viewed one's emotions. Very black and white. With extraordinarily little grey areas of emotions in between. Instead of flowing from one emotional state to the next, it seemed to be a manic leap. Most days in more of a Jekyll and Hyde scenario. With quick manic movements from extremely high to numerous exceptionally low times throughout the day.

As I searched, I came across the emotional scale many times, but I loved the way Abraham via Esther Hicks walked me through it. Her book *Ask and It Is Given* explained that by understanding the human emotion scale one had the ability to raise one's energetic vibration via climbing an emotional ladder. This similar emotional guidance scales are used throughout the psychological medical fields and are well documented to help guide people through trauma however this scale was new to me.

The Emotional Guidance Scale:
1. Joy/Appreciation/Empowerment/Freedom/Love.
2. Passion.
3. Enthusiasm/Eagerness/Happiness
4. Positive Expectation/Belief.
5. Optimism.
6. Hopefulness.
7. Contentment.
8. Boredom.
9. Pessimism.
10. Frustration/Irritation/Impatience.
11. Overwhelment.
12. Disappointment.

13. Doubt.
14. Worry.
15. Blame.
16. Discouragement.
17. Anger.
18. Revenge.
19. Hatred/Rage.
20. Jealousy.
21. Insecurity/Guilt/Unworthiness.
22. Fear/Grief/Depression/Despair/Powerlessness.

Ref. *Ask and It Is Given* pg. 114.

As I hang a photocopy of the emotion ladder on my fridge, I remind myself that emotions vary and many emotions which I thought to be the same were on vastly different levels. Even my now basic understanding of emotions brings a sense of relief and comfort to me. Especially understanding the emotion around anger and disappointment when it came to judging others and myself. I always felt they went hand in hand but as I read more into this process. Anger is one of the base low-vibration emotions but once I started to feel disappointment, I am actually raising my vibration and not making it worse. Working my way up through my emotions allows these emotions their own space ultimately raising my energetic vibration and mood.

As a ladder is a structure consisting of a series of bars or steps between two upright lengths of wood, metal, or rope, used for climbing up or down something. Loving and resonating with our emotions indeed feels like climbing a ladder making perfect sense to me as I have the ability to climb higher or to quickly slide downward from an unseen event.

The movement up the ladder of emotions can sometimes be slow and methodical, almost predictable. As I climb higher towards gratefulness and love with purpose. Those moments of simple joy felt-as I climbed my way to the top feeling the rush of peace and satisfaction. Easily brought on by simple moments such as this morning's walk as I bask in the warmth of the sun on my face watching the geese gracefully landing on the lake's surface.

While other times a slight shift in circumstances such as my child snapping a rude comment back to me will send me swiftly sliding down. Swiftly down like someone lubed up this emotional ladder with little to no ability to stop. Shooting me down at rocket speed. Down to the ground level, spraining my ankle on impact. Ok, maybe just spraining my pride or ego on impact. Fully committing to feeding into the fear as I top the event off with an even ruder response amplifying and feeding into additional negative behaviours.

As I start to delve into the emotional ladder, I feel it is all well and good to be aware of the many steps our emotions move through but what now. What does one do with all these emotions? Especially on days that I feel stuck on a particular emotion which I know does not feel particularly good and is feeding my shitty attitude.

Reality check-in: Day 279

Mind check-in:

Need to find a tool to help work through stuck emotions.

Body check-in:

Taking much better care of myself. Eating well. Exercising.

Spirit check-in:

I now seem to be very aware of my energy and emotions. Especially the negative ones.

As I find myself once again standing at the fridge staring at the emotion ladder pinned there. I am beginning to realise that each time I look at it I seem to learn something else about myself. My eyes move up and down the emotional ladder trying to get a better understanding. Understanding this morning's emotion of boredom is more of a neutral emotion. An emotion which has the ability to go up the emotional ladder with inspiration or down with self-pity and regret.

With the boredom of life came a need for silence. As boredom had spurred on many emotions of guilt, negative talk and the need to keep busy at all costs. I decided that today was as good of a day to try to be positive or at least attempt to silence the negative talk. Silence is the absence of ambient audible sound or the state of having ceased to produce any sound.

At first, the silence felt very uncomfortable almost as if I was being forced to sit in an empty room with a stranger. An uncomfortable silence of being judged not really sure what to do with myself or even how to hold my own body. It took many attempts as emergency tasks like doing the dishes and putting a load of laundry to wash forced me out of my silence. Trying to distract me from allowing a silent moment to unfold as I observed how and what I was sending my thoughts on.

Once the uncomfortable feeling passed and I realised that I was not going to die, explode or run for my life. Instead, a wave of relief washed over me. A wave that began to shed light on all the amazing things unfolding before my eyes without me exerting any effort at all, but just by sitting in silence and allowing.

These simple two to three minutes allowed life to slow down almost stop like I was able to pause all stress and tension that may have been building. I began to see examples in my own behaviour starting to soften and find peace.

Each morning, I realised that my soul was craving the peace found in silence. Especially the silence of my mind. Silence had the ability to create the space I needed to breathe. To disconnect and settle into the now. Lately, life had become extremely focused on tasks completed and pleasing others. So, a need to find a lasting solution was imminent. But how? What other ways could I create silence? Where else could I find it?

"As you think thoughts that feel good to you.

You will be in harmony with who you really are". — Abraham Hicks

When I think of silence I immediately think of meditation. I had dabbled over the years in many different types of meditation. One thing was for sure. I was not particularly good at it. Often any meditation longer than twenty minutes resulted in me nodding off or full-on sleeping. As I delved out of the conventional meditation styles of sitting lotus pose for one hour, I sparked a newfound hope for meditation. A creative spark of searching, implementing, and sharing all different types of meditations became my mission.

If I found a meditation that I loved and used I created a video. Only as I uploaded a new video today, I realised what an amazing tool our YouTube channel had been for us personally. Funny how it literally took us making one hundred and twelve videos for me to realise that all these videos we created were not just to make a positive ripple for others but for our very own mental wellbeing. Furthering my personal growth journey. Growth of learning a new skill. Growth of being creative. Growth of listening my needs.

Reflecting on the sheer relief I had found from creating. For if I found a breathing meditation helpful, I made a breathing meditation video. If I found mindfulness helpful, I made a mindfulness video. Everything from self-hypnosis to the pomodoro technique, inspired a video to be made. Even creating a video for our daughter who found looking at cute animals helpful as it relieved her stress.

Holy shit moment one thousand! Boredom did spur on creativity. If I was never bored, would I have ever created positive video content? Nope, I would have said, 'I do not have time for that.' Thankfully in all this chaos of covid, lockdowns, vaccines and social distancing it also brought about extensive personal time. Extensive personal time causing all types of emotions, boredom being one of many.

Creating positive content began to open my eyes to trust and love. Trust that there are positive people out there, who are looking for the same goal. No longer worried that someone is out to get me or take something from me. Opening myself up to all the positive energy that is out there in this big scary world. A big scary world which I once thought of as a world of trust no one, deadly viruses are out to get me and that all strangers are murderers or paedophiles. Instead, it became a journey of how I can reach as many people as possible, strangers and all in a positive way.

CHAPTER 13

The taste of disappointment

Spit the damn gum out. My sister Sue and I were talking today about how frustrating work had been for me lately. She shared a gum-chewing analogy she had recently heard about. A view which shed light on disappointment and our ability or inability for that fact, to let things go. Especially the negative minor issues in life. Hashing over events or conversations that went wrong, over, and over in our minds.

What was said? What should have been said? How someone acted? How someone under or overreacted? The list goes on in the negative state of holding onto something that is no longer serving a purpose or need.

This incessant need of rehashing resembled the state of chewing gum for far too long. Sure, at first, talking about all the new juicy details may release some type of satisfaction.

Relishing in the full emotional release over this new fresh experience. Justifying our feelings and need to express ourselves.

However, as the flavour dissipates, we continue to keep chewing and hashing over all the details. Usually over and over in our mind or to anyone who will listen. Allowing it to consume us. Feeding and relaxing into the negative energy flow fuelling the non-forgiver.

Continuing to chew through all the now stale details. Day after day, over and over, flavourless. That is unless we are able to bring ourselves into the present moment. To stop and observe. Realising as we come into the present moment that there is no satisfaction left. No sweet flavour. Just a nagging pain in your jaw and the bland taste of disappointment.

For me, the very real connection of how I seemed to chew the shit out of something that bothered me was glaringly apparent as I started to resonate with this chewing gum analogy. Realising that it is indeed about choice. Choice of thoughts, choice of words, choice of actions and of course a choice to just spit the damn gum out.

This metaphor sparked my spirit with the hope that I would now see my conditioned state of talking and thinking of stale feelings, thoughts, or issues to the death. Hashing it over and over. Never spitting it out. Never getting rid of it. Leaving me feeling unsatisfied and exhausted.

Almost as if I can literally feel my sore jaw from the relentless gnawing thoughts that had been circling in my mind. Such an inspiring lesson and visualization which I still use today to help shut down my thoughts while trying to create a little silence and space for myself.

I love these moments when the universe presents ideas and people to me at the perfect moment, pointing me in the right direction for positive growth.

"The art of conversation lies in listening". — Malcolm Forbes.

As I began searching into my need to judge and examine each and every interaction that I had in life sometimes to the death of it. I realised it was less about the reasoning and more about the listening and hearing what was actually happening than what I perceived as happening. Which resulted in a lot less rehashing and chewing over every word or action that pissed me off.

With the focus on understanding my thoughts being input into my mind every day came the desire to look at the output as well. The way I interact, spoke and did things for other people. This began my informal study of the art of conversation.

After all, "They say there is a real art form to conversation". Whoever "they" are.

The art of listening. The art of speaking. The art of storytelling. Even delving into the art form of being in the present moment in order to really absorb what the person is saying. To formulate thoughtful considerate comments to contribute to the conversation. By finding the perfect balance between speaking and listening, contributing, and learning.

After all, just because I thought it did not mean I needed to say or do it. Focusing on the importance of my words and how I contribute to the conversation. Did my replies have value? Was it kind? What was the topic? Was the conversation positive or negative? How did I feel after the conversation?

While observing the way I communicate with others I realise that everyday conversations had the ability to greatly affect my energy and mood. My attention is brought back to the simple fact that during most conversations I was more worried about pleasing others than pleasing myself with positive energy. Even if it meant going against my own gut reactions. A gut which was yelling, hey it is time to hang up. You are lowering your energy to match this conversation, and after three attempts to raise the conversation's energy level with no success, hang up the damn phone. But no. I ignore my gut reaction to hang up. Instead allowing myself to spiral onto the pity-party band wagon. Taking part in now talking about my own one shitty circumstance that happened this week. Instead of the ninety-nine other amazing little things I could have possibly talked about.

As I take a mental note, I add mindful conversation onto my list of to-do's.

Reality check-in: Day 301

Mind check-in:

Finding a need for balance between thinking and speaking.

Body check-in:

Feeling fairly good today. Stronger each day.

Spirit check-in:

Signs of being able to create joy.

As my husband, Kevin and I sat around this evening we talked at great length about our own conversational techniques. How we both wanted to listen more to our gut and care less about pleasing others by joining in. We discussed the stale gum analogy and how it shed light on our own thought patterns. What we thought we could improve upon in our own lives.

Then partake in a few laughs. As Kevin reminds me of another thought pattern habit that affected my conversation skills. One I am fully aware of but still do from time to time. The habit of being quick to blurt out things just to make sure I did not forget. Even if it meant it had nothing to do with the conversation at hand. Letting my mind take over. My husband enjoys calling this state of blurting "I love lamp". Lost in my own world. I was fully aware of my 'I love lamp' syndrome.

Reminding me to focus on the present moment instead of letting my mind have its own little side conversation hashing over details of task lists or jobs around the house. In the past, this would have been easy for me to take offence and may have even turned into a full-blown fight after taking insult to his comment. Turning it into a negative judgement fest focused back onto Kevin to somehow create an equal size insult wound. However, I knew his comment was centred from love. Love and humour which is the best learning tool for growth.

Observing, not judging as it presented an idea or need for change with love.

"I have always said that everyone is in sales. Maybe you don't hold the title of salesperson, but if the business you are in requires you to deal with people, you, my friend, are in sales". — Zig Ziglar

Sold refers to a person or organization interested in acquiring the offered item of value through the form of buying and selling which is understood to be two sides of the same "coin" or transaction. As we are all in a constant state of selling or buying something. Whether it be goods, ideas, concepts, or beliefs.

We are either the salesman or the buyer.

Tending to lean and gravitate towards goods, ideas, concepts, or beliefs that we already agree with. Whether you want to relate to it or not. Being a salesperson is a skill all in itself... What? I pause the podcast as I have a full-on disagreement in my mind, that I most certainly am *not* a salesman.

While my mind slams shut with a bang. I am left wondering why I am getting so defensive. Stop. Observe without judgement.

Of course, my past conditioning is playing a big part in this reaction. An emotional reaction that is somehow being sold to is being taken advantage of. I am certainly not trying to sell anyone. Vibrates through my mind knowing that a "key reset" is needed right about now.

I take a deep breath, striking my hands together in front of my face, palms over my closed eyes. My inner ninja breaks me out of my present state. This gesture also takes me out of my mind and into my body. Bringing my awareness to my breathing. Now allowing my breath to be the key. I sense the stillness as I sit in darkness. A darkness that reminds me that this is pretty much what my mind is doing right now. Closed and blocked off. Slamming the door to any new viewpoints of being either the salesman or the buyer.

I take a few breaths; I tell myself that then when I open my hands and eyes my mind too will be open. Using my breath gives me the key to reopen my mind. Allowing me to connect with my spirit. To create some space. Space to breathe. Space and silence to see the path forward.

I open my eyes. Press play to continue listening to the podcast. Officially my mind is now open. Apparently so open that I realised I am one of the biggest salesmen around. Not to mention a very sceptical buyer who questions everything.

It all became abundantly clear as I finished listening. I sat contemplating how this new perspective could help me to grow. To grow in the mindset that we are all salesman and buyers.

Salesmen and buyers even within our very own homes. Selling the idea and need to get my kids off of tech with bedazzled alternatives which were definitely upsold. Bribing them with walks to the corner store or bike rides to the park, to selling them on the idea of how helping out around the house would turn them into an Olympic team player. Even selling them on the need to do well in school and that a great report card equals more opportunities.

As well as me being the sceptical buyer being sold by my own children as to why they should be allowed to stay up later or have that extra serving of ice cream. Life is very much all about selling and being sold to. Buying and being bought.

"Open your eyes to the beauty around you, open your mind to the wonders of life, open your heart to those who love you, and always be true to yourself". — Maya Angelou

Tonight, Kevin is super pumped to share a new show he has been watching on YouTube. I gravitate to his energy until I find out it is about two brothers and their friends living and sailing around the world. I already hate it and I have not even watched it yet.

If you are a close friend of mine, you know that I do love the water but only on calm days. I have been known to get motion sickness at the drop of a hat. Motion sick in the car. Motion sick at the amusement parks. Motion sick on the swing at the park. Motion sick even under the water. As flashbacks of my honeymoon come flooding back.

Kevin and I had just got married after our intimate wedding in Edmonton with a few close friends and family we jumped on a plane to Mexico.

In keeping things simple and small we wanted to spend the majority of our budget on the honeymoon and adventures. We booked a two-week all-inclusive trip to Puerto Vallarta to soak up the sun. One of the excursions was to take a group tour by boat to an island to scuba dive, chill, and have a romantic dinner on the beach.

Our day started with a mainland big boat ride. I thought I had it all figured out as we sat top side and faced forward to minimize the motion. As the boat bobbed up and down with the waves the attendant came around to ask who as going scuba diving. We eagerly raise our hands. This would be my first scuba diving adventure after a quick lesson in the hotel pool. He then asks us to make our way below deck to get on our wet suites on.

What? You want me to walk around! OK, I got this.

The sway of the boat was not good to say the least. I managed to make my way below deck, get the wet suit on and make my way back to the safety of my perch top side feeling extremely nauseated. I can do this. I repeated over and over in my head as I look around and see the thirty other guests.

However, as the boat docked my internal voice started to turn to, "I do not have this". Walking became running. As I ran off the boat asking, "is it better to get sick in the water or the trash can". He points to the trash can. I proceeded to project my lunch and possibly breakfast into the trash can, as all the other tourists filed off the boat. 'Are you ok now?' one of the staff asked me. 'We need to board that fishing boat right now,' as he points to the tiniest of fishing boats. I look back at Kevin and see the disappointment in his eyes.

'OK,' I said as I wobbled my way aboard. Trying to convince myself and Kevin that I was feeling better now that I got sick.

The boat begins to surf each wave rounding the corner to a calmer inlet. Relieved to see the calm water we stop, gear up and drop into the water. As we start to descend under the water the sudden sense of the waves and water pressure consumes me. I feel the motion sickness build up once more. I signalled to the guide that I was done, he signalled back five more minutes.

OK, I got this. I do right. I think I do, nope. I better signal him, again. I am *done*!

As he signals back five more minutes he looks into my eyes. This time it must have been the sheer panic in my eyes because he quickly turns and signals to Kevin and the rest of the divers that he will now be back in five minutes. As we start to ascend, I cannot hold on any longer and purge once again.

All I can say is thank goodness it is a one-way valve. Embarrassed but so relieved I make my way back onto the fishing boat. Kevin chuckles later recalling how I apparently chummed the waters making his day and that the fish spectacle was absolutely amazing. You're welcome.

Tonight, again! Kevin wants to watch this damn sailing show. His energy is so contagious I give in and agreed. If I can hurl while scuba diving, then watching a sailing show from the comfort of our couch is not going to kill me.

After all his energy and excitement are that of a little boy at Christmas. How could I say no? Little did I know that his incessant need to watch this sailing show would bring out his own personal dream of one day sailing around the world living on a sailboat.

My initial thought is, were you even the same man I spent our honeymoon with as there was no way in hell that I would survive on a sailboat. As we watched each episode my mind started to shift from when hell freezes over to maybe my body would adjust. Apparently, everyone gets their sea legs so can I.

So, night after night, spending our one hour of coveted chill time before bed binge-watching episodes of SV Delos and manifesting a life of travel and freedom on our own sailboat began. I realised it was not even about sailing it was about opening my mind up to new things. Whether it would be sailing or another adventure I loved just how open my mind was becoming to new, unexpected adventures.

Opening my mind up began to rewrite my programming and my very being. The act or result of writing new source conditioning to replace an existing negative thought. This whole sailboat business has brought about many questions. Questions about past belief systems and past restrictions that one still believes to be true. If I could open my mind up and rewrite past beliefs, then maybe I also had the ability to craft them into a new story for myself.

Frankly, this thought sparked a feeling in me that anything was possible.

Finding fun new tools to efficiently reprogram more of my past beliefs would now be added to my to-do list. Past negative beliefs such as life needs to be hard. Money and abundance are only for a select few. That people never change. The list goes on and on and so did my search for the right tool to help reprogram all the past conditioning that said that I cannot.

Cannot dream big, live big, achieve big, love big and give big.

CHAPTER 14

I am

I am what?

As I sort through the many layers of sadness on my journey to healing and finding my true self. I am reminded of the sheer number of layers that I have already worked through and how many more layers there are still to go.

Similar to an onion shedding each layer. Only to realise that this onion is magical and has an infinite number of layers. These infinite layers which make me think that getting to the centre is not really the goal anymore.

Instead shifting my goal to be present while each layer is being peeled back. Producing something new and fresh. Sure, these layers may create tears and hardship, but they may also create a delicious meal of joy to be feasted on. Feeling an even deeper need to trust that all these complex emotions all serve a higher purpose.

Now that I realise, I am more like an onion with infinite layers as I am peeling them back it opens up my mind to many more ah moments. Moments which seem to shift me in such a positive way it is hard to put into words.

Delving deeper into the understanding of oneness. An understanding that we all have a light within. As I add in this "I am" simple yet powerful statement into my daily pep talks and my thoughts, joy surfaces with much more ease.

Constantly reminding myself that I am worthy. I am valued. I am enough. I am excited about how easily things come to me. I am able to pick myself up, again and again if needed. I am willing to try again knowing that I am creative and loving. As I flow with each mood that comes my way. I cannot help but smile today at just how proud and how far this year has taken me.

All this, "I am" talk has got me wondering about my life's purpose. Reminding me the purpose of life is not a job it is a feeling, and connections made. A feeling that I am starting to understand, when I am in alignment with my true self my spark could be felt. With purpose came my intentions. Intensions regarding the impact I wanted to make on myself and on others. Caring less about expectations and more about intentions.

Reminding myself to keep in mind a few key questions. What are my intentions of my thoughts, my words, my actions? Are my intentions coming from high or low rung on the emotion ladder? How charged are my emotions? What am I attracting? What tools can I use daily?

Two karmic buckets.

Karma, also known as the law of attraction, you get what you give. Either way, it all comes back to you. What could two buckets have to do with Karma, you may be asking?

A simple visualization regarding energy and the law of attraction became crystal clear when one uses two buckets.

Let's just say you are given two buckets. One bucket for all your negative thoughts, words, and actions and another bucket for all your positive thoughts, words, and actions.

Throughout the day take mental note of as many thoughts, words, and actions as you can. Visualize that with each thought, word, or action it is represented by a stone and depending on if it was negative or positive this stone would be placed into each respective bucket.

This is where the law of attraction comes in.

As you lay in bed at night reflecting on how full each bucket is, visualize yourself then placing these two buckets outside your front door.

In the morning Karma rings the doorbell to deliver your exact same buckets.

If my bucket was filled chock-full to the brim with negative stones, then it is very likely I am in for a rough day or week. Reflecting back on some of the roughest weeks I had ever encountered and wondered just how many nights of negative buckets filling it took-to get to this present state.

You see if my bucket only contained a few negative stones then I knew things had the potential to change in a positive way. Tasks became easier to complete. Family became way less annoying. I became way more loving.

For the first few days, I just observe without judgement as I filled the two buckets with each thought, word, and action I had that day. Mentally noting the stones being dropped-into its rightful bucket, positive or negative. At the end of my day, I would remind myself to assess the level which these two buckets possessed.

As each day passes. The realization that the fullness of the bucket was my output of energy for the day. This simple knowledge had finally made a lasting impression of the impact of what karma was. The true potential of what my energy input and output actually did.

Once again karma was a choice not a situation of circumstances taking us along for the ride. Positive energy and negative energy which I choose to order using an efficient overnight amazon delivery or sometimes delayed by using snail mail. Either way, I had finally understood that what I put out there always and I mean always came back to me.

They say, "karma can be a bitch". I say, "karma is a badass teacher". A teacher who shows you the potential for pure joy, and love, not to mention the potential to give you an old-school spanking if needed.

"You cannot nor need to fix yourself. Instead, just be and live the person you want you to be". — Abraham Hicks.

I am.

I am tool of repeating, writing, and listening to positive affirmation is a simple yet effective way of reprograming one's self.

Whether it be through affirmations. Which I kept to a simple statement with a positive message like, "I am worthy". "I am loved". "I am enough".

Or listening to I am self-hypnosis that uses "I am", to retrain your conditioning.

With each "I am" that I delved into. It brought up many different emotions and negative conditioning that I had adapted over my lifetime. This became a time of retraining my base conditioning as I found that no matter how positive I wanted to be the negative conditioning of thoughts and words had been so ingrained that I knew I would need to work on my subconscious even when I slept. It began with listening to positive affirmations and repeating them throughout my day. I had them posted everywhere my laptop, fridge, and bathroom mirror just to remind myself that I was worthy and on the right path no matter what was happening around me.

"Knowing others is intelligent. Knowing yourself is true wisdom. Mastering others is strength. Mastering yourself is true power".

— Lao Tzu

I am supported.

Almost all the mentors this far in my journey had no idea who I was and that they were mentoring me. Their focus on being true and making a positive impact with the knowledge that they had was so inspiring. It had cleared a path for me to see how amazing helping others and spreading positive energy truly was. This inspiration came to me in so many forms, through their books, inspirational cards, YouTube videos, blogs, training sessions, meditation classes and audiobooks. I found that these outside resources helped my personal growth exponentially. I have cited and given my gratitude to them at the end of this journey.

Whenever I found myself to be in a funk, I would ask the universe to show me what I needed today to help me grow and guide me on a path of positive energy and direction. The universe has many ways of showing us the way if you listen and are open. Sometimes it comes in an unexpected video popping up when my videos app was not even open. Or a stranger mentioning a book or inspirational quote. Even pulling the perfect card from my super attractor deck enabled me to shift my vibration.

A shift–that opened me up to receiving. Even as I drove for a quick Costco run repeating over and over in my mind that I am open to receiving. I had decided with all this social distancing that our families could use a little pick me up. I created a cute little album with each family's pictures of their adventures or lack thereof this year. Covid masks and all. As I stood at the pickup counter waiting to pay the Costco employee only to have him state that my total owing is only twenty-five bucks. *What! Amazing! Start the car!* Is my first thought.

I then find myself explaining that I would love to only pay the twenty-five bucks however that amount might get him in trouble at the end of the night when they go to cash out and his till is over a hundred dollars short. He thanks me and comments that karma will pay me back tenfold and winks. With his wink and candour my spark ignites warmth within my chest. Funny how a single moment has the ability to fill one's heart. I finished up my shopping and then headed to my car. Doubting this warm feeling in my chest for a moment I think to myself was the universe trying to give me some financial abundance? Toying with the idea that I maybe should have just smiled and paid the twenty-five bucks.

I get home and share my little Costco event with Kevin, asking him if he would have just paid? My husband in all his wisdom reassured me that receiving and taking are two vastly different things. Doing the right thing and knowing that there is a right time to receive and not to take. So, thank you, Kevin. Thank you for challenging me to be the best version of myself. Even when I doubt myself. We both evolve and change sometimes at vastly different speeds which really does not matter. Even in a relationship it is always better to receive than to take.

Receiving vs taking. The more I thought about this concept over the next few weeks I realised just how powerful this was. Why any simple gesture could be broken down into receiving verses taking. Clearly seeing in my own behaviour how sometimes I was taking. Taking was expecting acknowledgement or at the expense of another person. Charged up with the element of negative energy. Receiving was fluid and felt good leaving a lasting positive energy. With actions done with ease and no expectation of outcomes.

"I have found that if you love life, life will love you back". — Arthur Rubinstein.

I am allowing love to flow to me.

Over the next few days, I find myself in tears, a lot. Not full-out crying tears but rather small tears that streamed out of the corner of my eyes. My first thought is that there must be something wrong with my eyes, but no. I had no pain in my eyes. I was not over-tired. Quite the contrary I felt well-rested and energized. In fact, I had been having an amazing week even despite all the chaos happening in the world around me. These weird little tears still seemed to stream down my face at random times throughout my day. At first, I could not figure out why. Every time the tears flowed, I had been thinking, saying, or imaging something positive and amazing.

Sweet baby Jesus! Could this be. Could I be feeling happiness within? But it was more than just happiness. This was so different. It was actual joy. Joy that was not due to a specific action or reaction to anything in particular. Rather realising in the stillness of gratitude and awareness of the present moment. As this exciting realization settled in, and I embraced this glorious feeling the tears of joy stated to slowly flow out of the corners of my eyes. Is it possible to open myself up even more? To really feel it.

Allowing and giving myself the permission to just let go. Ultimately resulting in a few moments of a full-on ugly cry. Mixed with some weird laughing which made me laugh even more as I twirled around in my living room hugging myself spinning in circles. Well holy shit this really is a thing. I heard of people talk that if you embraced joy in the purest sense of the present moment it would be life changing. And damn it, it was!

Joy is a word used to denote a feeling of extreme happiness and cheerfulness, usually referring to intense delight in relation to one's sense of well-being rather than to one's mere personal pleasure.

As I open myself up to connecting each day with the universe. I feel my purpose grow. Not a purpose of a physical job or thing I needed to work toward. More of a purpose to create a positive mindset so that I can make a positive ripple of energy for myself and others. Constantly asking myself what can I do today to help, to connect to the universal life force? A life force which has that ability to make a difference.

It really does not matter how or what you believe in if the end result is believing in yourself to make positive change. We all have an ability to get there in our own time and manner. No matter how big or small it is still all equal. Positive is still positive. Because frankly, who doesn't want to relish in the feeling that positive energy brings?

The kind of energy that sends shivers up your spine a face splitting smile, or a tear of joy to your face. With an emotional overload shifting into a beautiful steady flow of energy. So, therefore bake those cookies for your neighbour. Hold the door for your wife. Give yourself time to reset. Just keep giving. Giving and opening to the circle of receiving as that is what powers the give even stronger. Be the human you want to be.

"It is wise to direct your anger towards problems—not people; to focus your energies on answers—not excuses". — William Arthur Ward.

I am human.

Sure, sadness still makes its appearance once in a while making me aware that I am not living in the moment, reminding me to be present. A mindset of being present where sadness can and will be relieved by feeling the emotion then embracing gratitude for all the amazing things big and small.

As my understanding of unconditional love grew so did my patience and the space created between reactions. After all, if I were to judge every little thing that went wrong in life with a fine-tooth comb I would not get anywhere. We all do what we perceive as horrible things. We hurt people. We say things we do not mean. But after all is that not just what the human experience is all about. Coming here. Being born into a physical world. To experience love, hate, hurt, and adventure. In every truly horrible thing that has happened to me I can now say that it has made me stronger. Stronger to stand tall and hold my heart open. To be open to possibility and love. Yes, very shitting things can, did and will happen in a lifetime. But it is those times when things get quiet, and I am alone with myself I realise I am going to be ok. I can achieve better things for myself. I can persevere.

Reminding myself that I am.

With all this I am business I have spent delving into over the last few months I realise that the disconnect with my spirit was directly correlated with the universe. As my once flawed mindset was that the universe and I were separate much like two people. Now understanding that we are actually one in the same. A powerful oneness. Within each and every one of us as we possess and are connected with the same spark. We may forget that it exists or how to tape into it or of its very existence, however knowing that it truly is within creates the connection that all pure good intensions are possible without limitations or exceptions.

"The only person you are destined to become is the only person you decide to be". — Ralph Waldo Emerson.

Tonight, as I lay in bed, I realise that I was never meant to live a perfect life. To be perfectly happy all the time. But more importantly that I am here to experience all that physical life offers. Realising that as friction and sadness came, they serve a particularly important purpose. To guide and move me along an amazing path.

No longer living in fear that something is going to go wrong or not my way. More so as seeing friction as a map to something new. No longer greeting friction by slamming the door of my mind shut or being disappointed for acknowledging it. Instead, I am grateful for noticing friction and embrace it with unconditional love for myself. I accept myself for all that it is.

A creative force of energy with the ability to have a healthy and vibrant life. With an ability to deal and sense imbalance. Imbalance in the mind. Imbalance in the body. Imbalance in the spirit. Having the ability to take those cues of imbalance as a way to balance all three, creating a vibration that moves through every cell of my being with every breath. With every sip of water. With every hot shower. With every conversation. With every sunset watched. I drift off to sleep excited for what tomorrow will bring.

Reality check-in: Day 360

Mind check-in:

Realised today just how quiet my mind had the ability to become.

Body check-in:

Yeah baby, worked my way up to fifteen push-ups today.

Spirit check-in:

On a roll of connection and tapping in, feeling the love.

CHAPTER 15

365 days to heal

Day 365.
That faithful day finally came, three hundred and sixty-five, sweet baby Jesus, I made it.

I cannot believe that I actually committed the last three hundred and sixty-five days to healing and learning more about myself than I ever thought was possible. Today is a day of celebration and realization that my journey will always continue for as long as I am open to growth. That making it through three hundred and sixty-five days does not signal the end but the beginning.

The beginning of a new life and a newfound freedom of choices.

Choices which over the last year proved that they would and could be life-changing experiences. Changes that have taught me that I am capable of being anywhere and around anyone and still maintain a positive vibration.

Well, most of the time. After all, we are all human. Humans who have the ability to create positive and negative vibrations through this powerful attraction within each thought, each word, and each action.

In celebration this morning I remind myself of all the choices I have. That happiness is a choice. Love is a choice. Forgiveness is a choice. Anger is a choice. Even sadness is a choice.

As my three hundred and sixty-five days of healing ends, I reflect on the sheer growth that my body, mind and spirit have been through. With each high and each low. Each with their own purpose in shifting me onto an amazing path with infinite options to choose from.

At the start of this journey, I would have said it was all about being here to speak my truth of personal growth, in search of releasing gripping sadness.

However, as I documented and shared my journey over the past three hundred and sixty-five days, I realised it was so much more.

It was about serious gut-wrenching self-reflection which had an infinite payoff of self-growth, self-love, and self-confidence. Confidence that I am worthy of love, that I am good enough and that I do have a choice as I open my eyes to the gratitude of the day. I now know that even as the path seems to narrow and muddy up from time to time that I will always find my way. As I am no longer lingering in sadness and self-pity.

It has also been a year filled with so many emotions, so many releases and rapid personal growth. As I channel and tap into my true self, I realise that sadness did not have a deafening grip on me.

That it was me gripping tight to the sadness with a mind that was too afraid to see what would happen if I just let go. Thankfully this journey has empowered me to slowly loosen my grip on sadness and trust in the glorious release of many emotions.

I can finally see the true purpose of sadness, not with the purpose to torture oneself but to encourage me to move up a rung or two on the emotional ladder to greater things. Knowing that I was just exhausting myself by trying to cling to that one rung of sadness for extended periods of time. When actually those uncomfortable feelings of exhaustive sadness were merely a sign from the universe to keep moving up.

In moving forward even in the shittiest of circumstances, a spark of joy can be achieved. Leaving me most days able to see the potential in a situation. Acknowledging a love for my true self as I ignite my spark. The spark that ignites a fiery breath within me. Fuelling me with the courage and fierceness to look within as I release timelines and judgement by simply allowing myself to heal.

Therefore, if I could so graciously at to leave you with one little golden nugget of advice. Hopefully one little spark of hope. It would be to STAY OPEN.

Open to receiving. Open to getting to know yourself better. Open to observe your current behaviour and mindsets. Open to laughing at yourself by giving yourself time and unconditional love to apply all that comes along your way. Open to getting to know that little bitch or bastard within. Open to picking up the pieces.

Open to being amazing and ultimately hoping that somewhere amongst all these words some small spark of inspiration is felt.

As my true goal and intention of sharing my journey was to inspire a foundation for true self-love, and a strong belief in self-worth by awakening a spark.

✴

A spark from within myself, and hopefully for you too as you read about this journey. Remembering-that every little positive action causes a positive reaction so please spark, spark away!

To be continued...

Tool reference and gratitude.

Tools I used for awakening my spark and opening my mind:

Abraham (Ester Hicks). — *Ask and it is Given.*

Bob Proctor — *Mind Movies.*

Dr Bradley Nelson — *Emotion Code* for helping me learn how to release trapped emotions.

Dr Joe Dispenza — *Becoming Supernatural. Breaking the Habit of Being Yourself. You are the Placebo.*

Gabby Bernstein — for my buddy Sandra who gave me the *Universe has your back* book which changed the course of my life. Gabby for your truly inspiring book and your beautiful *Super Attractor Cards* which has carried-me through many rough days and difficult decisions.

Jake Ducey — *Self-Hypnosis* for helping to break past conditioning while I slept.

Jay Shetty — *Think Like a Monk.*

Regan Hilliar — For your endless empowerment of embracing feminine energy.

Rhonda Byrne — *The Secret.*

Christine — *Quantum Therapy.*

Tools I used for boosting my immune system and dealing with anxiety:

Mel Robbins — For your *5, 4, 3, 2, 1 Method*', Mel and her son's car banter on Instagram are priceless.

Robin Sharma — *Five a.m. Club.*

Wim Hof Method App — For helping me push past fear by using your insightful breathing, and cold therapy not to mention the reminder to just breathe mother fucker!

Tools I used for healing:

Balance Health Wellness Music — For giving me a positive outlet to create something positive in a time when the world was turned upside down.

Mei-Ian YouTube — Your angelic voice allowed for many, many shifts.

Mother Nature — Unconditional love.

Best for last *many, many, many thanks* to:

Kevin — For motivating me to go within.

Makayla — For reminding me daily that you should never take life too seriously and to continually feed creativity.

Spencer — For your old man's wisdom, witty jokes, and many stories.

Friends and family — For those who positively impacted and continue to support my journey.

Shelley and Heather — For your gracious edits and feedback.

My Parents — Diane and Al, it is through all my experiences that have made me the powerful woman I am today.

Covid dedication: To all those who lost loved ones and to those who have tirelessly worked through this pandemic my spark of light goes out to you.

Universe — For always and unconditionally being there for me.

Myself — For waking up and wanting more even if it meant in the darkness.

'Sparking the light that exists within you'.

Contract to myself:

To-Do-List: